HOW TO UNDERSTAND THE BIBLE

BY W. ROBERT PALMER

D1559950

HOW TO
UNDERSTAND
THE BIBLE

BY W. ROBERT PALMER

Study Course for Youth and Adults

College Press Publishing Company
Joplin, Missouri

International Standard Book Number: 0-89900-140-8

Formerly Published by Standard Publishing Co.
Cincinnati, OH 1965

Philip:

"Do you understand what you are reading?"

Ethiopian:

"How can I, unless someone explains it to me?"

—Acts 8:30,31

Foreword

Learning in our modern day has become exceedingly skillful and productive. Never before have the tools and methods of education been so refined. Man is now able to absorb an enormous amount of facts, successfully dissect truth from error, scientifically test all evidence, free his thinking from prejudice, draw conclusions that are amazingly accurate, and manifest a level of wisdom unsurpassed. This he can do, if he wishes to pay the price. The horizon of good thinking in all areas of life is at its greatest extent.

Now consider what all this means to the Christian and his Bible. The Scriptures have been preserved and restored to their original message with scientific precision. Thus, the Word of God stands ready to be grasped by anyone with the faith and desire to do so. No generation of disciples has a better opportunity than do we to know the thoughts of God as He revealed them down through the ages in the Bible record. What a grand thought! If the Bible student will but take every modern skill and technique of learning, and add to it his insatiable desire and faith to understand the word, he will know the mind of God as no other people have yet had the privilege of knowing it.

This little book is intended to help point the way to this end. It is the hope that these few suggestions, methods, and rules will prove practical to those who simply say, "I want to understand God's Word." In this regard, all of us at times can use help.

Then he opened their minds so they could understand the Scriptures (Luke 24:45).

Thus, if the user comprehends the Lord and His will a little better, and walks a little closer with the Lord, then this work has served its purpose.

. . . for the Lord will give you insight into all this (2 Timothy 2:7).

The greatest moment and point of contact is the meeting of two minds, God's and man's.

This is what the LORD says:
Let not the wise man boast of his wisdom
or the strong man boast of his strength
or the rich man of his riches,
but let him who boasts boast about this:
that he understands and knows me,
that I am the LORD, who exercises kindness, justice, and
    righteousness on earth,
for in these I delight,
                declares the LORD (Jeremiah 9:23,24).

CONTENTS

CHAPTER ONE

Before You Begin

"In the beginning God created . . . And God said . . ."
(Genesis 1:1,3).

As in any study, one must have a point of beginning. In mathematics we begin with a simple set of axioms. An axiom is a commonly accepted truth. By laying a foundation of self-evident truths, a system of mathematical exercises can be worked out resulting in logical and useful conclusions.

In like manner, we first need to outline some principles — nine simple facts in all. We shall not spend much time to prove these, for this would be a separate study of its own. We merely begin at these points because they all must be firmly fixed in our minds before we can begin to understand the Bible.

God Has Spoken

This must be first. The whole Bible is based on this truth. Open the Scriptures at the very beginning and read. Just as we become aware of the universe around us and conclude that "God is," we read from this book to find out who God is. Notice: "In the beginning God created . . ." (Genesis 1:1), and we do not read much farther until ". . . God said . . ." (Genesis 1:3).

Is it not plain common sense that the God who made us, with all the righteousness and power of the divine Creator, would also talk to us? Is it not equally sane for all of us to want to know what He has said?

"In the past God spoke to our forefathers through the prophets at many times and in various ways, but in these last days he has spoken to us by his Son . . ." (Hebrews 1:1,2).

The Bible Is a Revelation of His Will

The Bible is not man's effort to reach up to God, but God's effort to reach down to man. If you are a young person, consider the school you attend. We do not go to all the expense and time to develop a school system just to enable one to go to class to show off what he has learned by himself. Instead, textbooks and trained teachers are combined to impart to a student all the needful time-tested truths possible. That is to help him to think rightly about the physical world in which he lives. Similarly, when it comes to God and spiritual truth, man has everything to learn and nothing to teach. Thus, the Bible is the product of God teaching us what we cannot learn by ourselves.

There is ample proof that the Bible is that record of God speaking to man. Consider the marvelous unity of the Scriptures (some forty different writers produced sixty-six books over a span of about fifteen hundred years), its overwhelming miracles, the abundance of irrefutable prophecies, the grand scope of the whole book, the powerful influence of its truth, its scientific and historical accuracy, the unexcelled moral tone, and the genuine uniqueness of its material, and you have evidence piled upon evidence that this is God's Word.

Of course, this is what the Bible has always claimed for itself. "For prophecy never had its origin in the will of man, but men spoke from God as they were carried along by the Holy Spirit" (2 Peter 1:21). Listen to the Apostle Paul when he said, ". . . what I am writing to you is the Lord's command" (1 Corinthians 14:37). Hundreds of times the Bible makes such claims of inspiration.

The Bible Has Been Accurately Translated

Yes, the original Old Testament was written in the Hebrew and Aramaic languages, and the New Testament in the Greek. If we cannot communicate intelligibly in these tongues, then the next best thing must be done. The Bible must be translated into the language we know and commonly speak. This practice makes it possible today to read the works of such great writers as Homer (writing in Greek), Plato (Greek), Virgil (Latin), Julius Caesar (Latin), Dante (Italian), Tolstoy (Russian), Guy de Maupassant (French), Omar Khayyam (Persian), etc.

With all of our wisdom and modern techniques, this task has been done for us in a very clear and thorough manner. Just think, from the original languages of the Scriptures, thousands of words have been translated into our everyday English language. And we can be assured that the Bible we read today is faithful to that which the Lord first had recorded through the guided efforts of inspired men. Floyd E. Hamilton says of the New Testament, "There is no doubt that we have the text . . . as it came from the hands of the original writers, in 999 words out of every thousand, and that the one out of every thousand about which there is still doubt, in no instance affects the meaning of any vital doctrine of the Church."[1]

The Bible Is Infallible/Inerrant

The Scriptures as they were originally written by inspired men were free of error. We can trust the Scriptures completely!

Have you not had some doubt about the trustworthiness of some writings or sayings of man? Have you not found some things that are not one hundred percent worthy of

---

[1] *The Basis of the Christian Faith* (3rd. ed.; New York: Harper & Brothers Publishers, 1946), p. 203.

your complete trust? Often it is simply due to the human weakness of mind and flesh.

This is not true of the Bible. It is unique in the real sense of the word — none other like it. It stands out in sharp contrast to all the works of men. The great statesman, W.E. Gladstone, spoke well when he said, "The Bible is stamped with specialty of origin, and an immeasurable distance separates it from all competitors." Remember that all confusions, errors, and contradictions emanate from the mind of man, not from the Word of God.

Within the last century there has arisen a relatively new science — archaeology. This is the study of the various types of remains of the past civilizations of the world. As these items are unearthed, catalogued, and studied, it is interesting to note this overwhelming fact: in all of the thousands of discoveries, the Bible has yet to be shown inaccurate on any given point of history. To the contrary, archaeology has developed an abundance of evidence supporting and illuminating the text of the Bible. "The law of the LORD is perfect, reviving the soul. The statutes of the LORD are trustworthy, making wise the simple" (Psalm 19:7).

The Bible Is Complete and Final

Any record of importance, though it is true, is not perfect, if it does not give sufficient information.

For example, suppose you sought directions on how to get from your house to a certain city, and someone very thoughtfully drew a neat map and carefully explained the route you should take for three-fourths of the journey. Though this help would not be worthless, nevertheless it would be imperfect and leave much to be desired. As a matter of fact, an incomplete message is not a clear message at all. Man must have the complete story, all the necessary truth, or else he will be misled. There must be no sequel.

Study the entire Bible content. Notice the grand theme of

the divine-human relationship and you will see that it is final. There is completeness in every divine plan, an ending to the long story of man, an ultimate goal to every purpose of God, perfection in the life and sacrifice of God's Son, a perfect pattern for the faith and life of the Christian, and final glory in the system of salvation for man.

What else is there to say? Nothing! Where else is there to go? Nowhere! Truly, in the Bible we have "the faith that was once for all entrusted to the saints" (Jude 3).

Therefore, the Bible is God's complete record for your life. You cannot outgrow it. It is not merely a key to truth — it is the truth. It contains all that you need to know about life here and the hope of life in the hereafter.

Paul wrote to Timothy:

> And how from infancy you have known the holy Scriptures, which are able to make you wise for salvation through faith in Christ Jesus. All Scripture is God-breathed and is useful for teaching, rebuking, correcting and training in righteousness, so that the man of God may be thoroughly equipped for every good work (2 Timothy 3:15-17).

The Bible Is Intelligible

You receive a letter through the mail. What are your first thoughts? Do you not automatically conclude that some person had some thoughts, wrote them down on paper, mailed them to you, and your first response is to open the letter and read it? There is little other value in a message. It is not a charm; neither is it to be framed nor worn, but is to be read and understood.

The Bible is first, last, and always a message. The mere possession of it, or even a casual glance at its contents, does not provide one with some kind of a magical blessing. God has something to say to man that is important. Through many inspired persons God has directed it to the mind of man. As Alexander Campbell once wrote, *"God has spoken by men, to men, for men.* The language of the Bible is then, *human* language."[2]

Read the Bible! God has always wanted man to hear and understand Him. He has used every means known to human communication of thought to accomplish this. "For everything that was written in the past was written to teach us, so that through endurance and the encouragement of the Scriptures we might have hope" (Romans 15:4).

The Bible is a revelation; and a revelation is an uncovering of that which is hidden, so that it may be clearly seen. A crowd gathers around a statue. When it is unveiled for the first time, the public beholds the beauty of the long-awaited masterpiece. It is no longer a mystery. Through sense perception the audience understands what it is. God did the same with a body of truth, which man could not discover by himself, but which man can now understand for the first time. The mysteries of God, necessary for man's well-being, are now open and plain to man.

The Bible Can Be Understood by Man

Man is a rational being, made in God's image to think and to reason. By exercising this divine right, man is able to read the mind of God — that portion which God revealed. No other created being has this privilege.

Is it not reasonable that God, in communicating with His children, would call upon man's highest faculty — the power of reason? Reason surpasses emotion, instinct, intuition, etc. Why use a lesser or more undependable trait for such an important matter? Why listen for the sound of an enemy when you have radar; or why trust your feelings about health, when you can submit to an accurate scientific diagnosis?

The mind is not our God, but it should be used to know God. In building our house of divine knowledge we must use

---

[2]Alexander Campbell, *Christianity Restored* (Rosemead, CA: Old Paths Book Club), p. 22.

our mental power as a tool to understand the meanings of God's blueprint (the Bible). "Consequently, faith comes from hearing the message, and the message is heard through the word of Christ" (Romans 10:17).

Two children were playing on a hillside when they noticed that the hour was nearing sunset. One said wonderingly, "See how far the sun has gone! A little while ago it was right over that tree, and now it is low down in the sky."

"Only it isn't the sun that moves, it's the earth. You know, Father told us," answered the other.

The first one shook his head. The sun did move, for he had seen it; and the earth did not move, for he had been standing on it all the time. "I know what I see," he said triumphantly.

"And I believe Father," said his brother.

The first boy had permitted himself to be completely mastered by his own powers of reason and observation; while the second boy used his reason and memory to direct him in the truth as revealed by his father. We should let the mind then be servant to the revealed mind of God in all spiritual truth.

Understanding the Bible is a duty. When God speaks, we are to listen and understand. There is no alternative.

God never expects the impossible of man. The Bible is filled with examples of this teaching. The Word is never grievous to hear. God is perfect in holiness and mercy, as well as justice. He would never demand that we know the unknowable. The apostle Paul wrote what was revealed to him, "In reading this, then, you will be able to understand my insight into the mystery of Christ" (Ephesians 3:4). Again, he said to young Timothy, "Reflect on what I am saying, for the Lord will give you insight into all this. . . . Do your best to present yourself to God as one approved, a workman who does not need to be ashamed and who correctly handles the word of truth" (2 Timothy 2:7,15). This implies that we can handle the Word "incorrectly" — and leads us to the next point.

The Bible Correctly Understood Is Authoritative

If our tool of the mind should ever be dulled by such weaknesses as prejudice, wishful thinking, superstition, preconceived notions (or any of the violations of logic and common sense), then our understanding will be impaired. In turn, to that degree the authoritative voice of God will be weakened. This is what Peter meant when referring to the writings of Paul in Scripture:

> His letters contain some things that are hard to understand, which ignorant and unstable people distort, as they do the other Scriptures, to their own destruction (2 Peter 3:16).

The end is more deadly than many suppose. We should ever be alert to the distinction of truth and error.

The truth is always there for those who seek it. Jesus taught this principle as He stood face to face with those who loved error and would not embrace the truth. Therefore, they refused Him as their Lord.

> You will be ever hearing but never understanding;
> you will be ever seeing but never perceiving.
> For this people's heart has become calloused;
> they hardly hear with their ears,
> and they have closed their eyes.
> Otherwise they might see with their eyes, hear with their ears, understand with their hearts and turn, and I would heal them (Matthew 13:14,15).

Back in the sixth century when ignorance, tradition, and superstition were prevalent in the world, there arose a society of believers, like a rose rising out of a swamp. A man named Columba set up a school of the Scriptures on the small island of Iona, just off the coast of Scotland. Here the people were taught to know, understand, and obey the teachings of the Bible. Historians tell us that for a brief time there lived a people who knew only the works of love, worship and righteousness as taught in the Scriptures — their sole authoritative guide.

The Authority of the Bible Demands Submission

There is no other conclusion. This progression of thought leads us to one point: we must now, without delay, embrace with full faith and obedience all that God says. As we hold the Bible in our hands, we stand before God. Paul says:

> God "will give to each person according to what he has done." To those who by persistence in doing good seek glory, honor, and immortality, he will give eternal life. But for those who are self-seeking and who reject the truth and follow evil, there will be wrath and anger. There will be trouble and distress for every human being who does evil: first for the Jew, then for the Gentile (Romans 2:6-9).

What have faith and obedience to do with the understanding of the message? When one begins to rebel against the truth, in the process of learning it, he will soon find the true understanding of its meaning slipping from his grasp or out beyond his reach. This is a Bible principle. More than once the Lord has withheld spiritual understanding from the wise and prudent who were often arrogant and rebellious, while revealing it to humble children who have lovingly trusted and obeyed Him. Read Matthew 5:8; 13:14,15; Acts 7:51-53; 2 Corinthians 4:3,4; 2 Thessalonians 2:8-12; 2 Timothy 4:3,4.

Questions for Review

1. How has God spoken to man?
2. It took how many authors about how many years to write the Bible?
3. The Bible was originally written in what languages, and why must it be translated?
4. What relatively new science has helped confirm the accuracy of the Bible, and how?
5. What does the word "revelation" mean?
6. Does God expect you to understand the Bible? Why?
7. Why is obedience to the teachings of the Bible important to your understanding of it?

Assignments for Study

1. Remembering that there are hundreds of references in the Bible that refer to its inspiration, ask each student to find at least five.
2. Have several students study and relate in class an archaeological story that graphically supports the accuracy of a Bible narrative or claim.

Topics for Discussion

1. If the Bible were incomplete, discuss what effect this would have on our understanding of God's truth.
2. Give examples of how misunderstandings of the Bible message lead people to actually do things that are wrong.

CHAPTER TWO

Tools You Will Need

"You diligently study the Scriptures because you think that by them you possess eternal life. These are the Scriptures that testify about me"
(John 5:39).

The Importance of This Task for You

You are about to enter upon one of the most blessed and rewarding experiences of all mankind — studying the Bible. This book is no mere collection of human opinions, theories, or fancies. The Bible is a book of great facts from God. These are life-and-death facts, truths that pertain to your salvation. They must be understood, for much is at stake. You must study so that His thoughts will become your thoughts, and that you may understand His will for you.

As R.A. Torrey wrote,

> This Book makes men wise with the wisdom that is golden, the wisdom that brings eternal salvation. No one can study this Book aright, no matter how ignorant he may otherwise be, without being possessed of that priceless wisdom that means eternal life. No other book has the power to make us acquainted with God and with his Son, Jesus Christ, that this book has. Oh, study the Book that shows the way to eternal life; make it in your own experience "the engrafted word, which is able to save your souls" (James 1:21).

A serious warning was issued by Jesus to those who hear

the Word and fail to understand it. "When anyone hears the message about the kingdom and does not understand it, the evil one comes and snatches away what was sown in his heart" (Matthew 13:19).

Understanding the Bible is a job. You do not inherit understanding, nor is it given you, nor does God cast a magical spell over you. It takes study. Study, among other things which this book shall list, takes tools. It seems fitting then, at this point, for us to suggest twelve practical tools every Bible student should have.

A Bible

The first need is a *Bible*, but not just any Bible. This is important! The writer counted thirty-one different Bibles in his study, with nearly as many different uses. Many may be convenient to carry, pretty to look at, expensive to buy, but not suited to study. Secure a bold, clear print Bible, one that is easy to use and inviting to read. Too many cause fatigue and eyestrain just to read, not to mention study. The type should be large enough for marking, and there should be margins for notes. A stiff board cover (like an ordinary book) is recommended, with heavy paper pages.

A Bible Concordance

This is nothing more than an alphabetical arrangement of all (or most) of the words of the Bible. This is most useful and saves hours of time for those many occasions in which you need to locate certain passages of Scripture. Simply look up a word (part of the verse desired), and the concordance will indicate where you may turn in the Bible to find your passage. This enables you to find a verse of Scripture when you remember a part of it, or even only one word of it.

A Bible Dictionary

This helps the student understand the meanings of Bible things, persons, places, events, laws, ordinances, mountains, rivers, cities, etc. It is not enough to use a modern dictionary, for this gives the present-day uses of terms. This is not what we want. We want the meanings of these terms in Bible times, and the meanings of the words that we no longer use.

Maps and Atlases

Maps and atlases are also essential to good study. The Bible record is an historical record. Thus, understanding is increased by locating and depicting the events of Scripture.

A Modern Language Bible

It is also good to select one or more reliable *modern speech Bibles*, and there are some excellent ones. Some of the better known modern versions include:

Revised Standard Version (the first of the modern spate of popular English translations, a bit dated now) (1952)
Amplified Bible (tries to give the exact shades of meaning by "amplifying" words with their synonyms) (1964)
Jerusalem Bible (translated into English from a French translation) (1966)
New English Bible (smooth-reading modern translation, with British spellings and some expressions) (1970)
Living Bible (a paraphrase of the old American Standard Version; not recommended for in-depth study.) (1971)
New Testament in Modern English (Phillips translation; paraphrase by a British scholar, not as loose a paraphrase as the Living Bible) (revised 1972)
New American Standard Bible (the most accurate to the original languages of all the modern versions, but this makes it read a little "rough" at times) (1977)
Today's English Version (from the United Bible Societies, originally developed to aid translators into other languages; also known as Good News for Modern Man, or the Good News Bible) (1976)
New King James Version (1982)
New International Version (1984)
New Jerusalem Bible (1985)
Revised English Bible (a revision of the New English Bible) (1989)

New Revised Standard Version (1989)
Contemporary English Version (the latest from the American Bible Society: NT, 1991, full Bible anticipated 1995)

We should be willing to use different versions in order to bring the original meaning of the word into the living language of our day. The truth of God does not change, even though the languages of men (the conveyances of that truth) do change with time. Such versions, therefore, can reveal fine shades of meaning, use more words to explain all the facets of meaning in a given word, and more accurately explain verb tenses and idioms. Any version that is true to the text and makes it more understandable is useful. The biggest objection to these versions is that often they are products of individual scholars and thus apt to be more biased. Also, it must be remembered that some translations are so "free" (Living Bible is a good example) that they practically become commentaries.

Books and Commentaries

Written by Men can be fallable

Select, with care, certain *books* and *commentaries*. This should often be done with help. A trustworthy student of the Bible could offer wise suggestions in the matter of selecting reliable commentaries. And then they should be used carefully, only as human aids.

Clark's

Time for Study

The next tool is *time*. You will never *find* time to really study the Bible — you will have to *take* time. We live in a busy age. For the average person there are more interests and duties than can be crowded into one's schedule. So it is a matter of budgeting one's time. One must apportion things according to their true worth and satisfaction. You will have to arrange for your study time, plan on it, hold to it, and exclude lesser things that hinder. Select the time when you are physically and mentally alert. Make a schedule. Then resolutely hold to it. This is good stewardship.

A Place to Study

Don't forget to select a good *place* for study. The room, the desk, the chair, the lighting, an atmosphere that aids concentration, and privacy to prevent distractions are not to be overlooked. There is merit in having a particular place to study the Bible.

A Plan of Study

It is also important that you pick out a *system* or *plan* of study. Never let it be aimless. There are many plans to follow. Here are a few: study books of the Bible verse by verse, persons of the Bible, doctrines (such as prayer, faith, sin), prophecies, promises, types (see p. 122), narratives, parables, miracles, Bible school lessons, midweek prayer meeting lessons, sermon studies, and word studies. Change your plan from time to time.

There is a good advantage for some "together" studying, such as husband and wife, two or three friends, brothers and sisters, and the immediate family. Try it!

Pencil and Paper

Next, get out *paper* and *pencil.* These will become two of the most useful tools in understanding the Bible. More about this is under the next item.

Good Study Habits

A strong emphasis should be placed upon the matter of developing good *study habits.* Many of our school systems are including this in the required studies for young people. Do you know how to study correctly? Many combine poor habits with good habits. We should emphasize not only the amount of study effort, but the direction of it as well. May we suggest four simple study habits that will help a student of the Bible?

1. *Read correctly,* since the main purpose of this practice is to understand. Reading the Bible is a method of inquiring into the truth as God has recorded it. Thus, there are a num-

The Divine Pattern for Unity

Unity in the Body of Christ

4 As a prisoner for the Lord, then, I urge you to live a life worthy of the calling you have received. [2]Be completely humble and gentle; be patient, bearing with one another in love. [3]Make every effort to keep the unity of the Spirit through the bond of peace. [4]There is one body and one Spirit– just as you were called to one hope when you were called– [5]one Lord, one faith, one baptism; [6]one God and Father of all, who is over all and through all and in all.

[7]But to each one of us grace has been given as Christ apportioned it. [8]This is why it[a] says:

"When he ascended on high, he led captives in his train and gave gifts to men."[b]

[9](What does "he ascended" mean except that he also descended to the lower, earthly regions? [10]He who descended is the very one who ascended higher than all the heavens, in order to fill the whole universe.) [11]It was he who gave some to be apostles, some to be prophets, some to be evangelists, and some to be pastors and teachers, [12]to prepare God's people for works of service, so that the body of Christ may be built up [13]until we all reach unity in the faith and in the knowledge of the Son of God and become mature, attaining to the whole measure of the fullness of Christ.

[14]Then we will no longer be infants, tossed back and forth by the waves, and blown here and there by every wind of teaching and by the cunning and craftiness of men in their deceitful scheming. [15]Instead, speaking the truth in love, we will in all things grow up into him who is the Head, that is, Christ. [16]From him the whole body, joined and held together by every supporting ligament, grows and builds itself up in love, as each part does its work. *Each member does his part*

Living as Children of Light

[17]So I tell you this, and insist on it in the Lord, that you must no longer live as the Gentiles do, in the futility of their thinking. [18]They are darkened in their understanding and separated from

[a]8 Or *God* [b]8 Psalm 68:18

ber of skills that should be involved as you proceed. They are asking, comparing, contrasting, exploring, concentrating, rereading, orientating, analyzing, memorizing, defining, and concluding.

2. Next is *marking* the Bible or *making signs* — drawing charts, graphs, pictures, etc. The value of seeing the truth is never to be underestimated. One student while in college developed a series of "markings" in school, and later came to use this system to great advantage as he studied the Bible. On the page opposite is a sample of various helpful markings that have proved most useful.

3. *Making notes and outlines* has a way of helping the student understand and retain what he understands. Also, he is more apt to be accurate. When a person writes down what he is learning, he can better distinguish, relate, and orientate the material. For example, see the outline of 1 Thessalonians, overleaf.

4. *Self-recitation* is also most important. Some professional educators claim that learning is at its best when much time is spent in reciting to oneself. It makes learning more thorough, causes the understanding to be clearer, and increases interest in the whole subject. You understand better that which you can tell or teach. Remember this threefold rule: learn to read, reflect, and recall.

Our understanding of the Bible will be greatly increased when we put into practice these scientific study habits.

An Alert Mind

Our final tool is the *human mind* — it is by no means the least significant. On the contrary, it is so vital to the whole subject that we devote a whole chapter to it. Moreover, this tool is deeply involved in all the material that follows.

Of course, if you have accepted the Lord, you are expected, yes, you are commanded, to study the Word with the intention of understanding it (2 Timothy 2:15). This alone is reason enough for all this discussion. How our ignorance

OUTLINE OF THE BOOK OF FIRST THESSALONIANS

PART ONE—Paul's relations with the Thessalonians,
    past and present   Chapters 1,2,3

  I. Paul's thanks for the Thessalonians   1:2-10
     A. When Paul expressed thanks (1:2-3)
     B. Things for which Paul expressed thanks (1:4-10)
        1. Their election (1:4-6)
        2. Their example (1:7-10)

  II. Paul's good record among the Thessalonians   2:1-16
     A. Paul's work among them (2:1-12)
     B. Thanks for the way they received the word (2:13-16)

  III. Paul's current dealings with the Thessalonians   2:17-3:10
     A. Paul's desire for personal visit hindered (2:17-20)
     B. Timothy sent (3:1-5)
     C. Joy upon Timothy's return (3:6-10)

Concluding prayer   3:11-13

PART TWO—Exhortations and teachings   Chapters 4,5

  I. The walk of the Christians   4:1-12

  II. The Lord's coming   4:13-5:11
     A. The dead in Christ and the Lord's coming (4:13-18)
     B. Times and seasons of the Lord's coming (5:1-11)
        1. Comes as a thief (5:1-3)
        2. Will not come to Christians as a thief (5:4-11)

  III. Practical Exhortations   5:12-22

Concluding prayer, commands, and benediction   5:23-28

displeases God (Hosea 4:6, 2 Thessalonians 1:7-9)!

But aside from this, let us consider the high privilege we have of understanding the Bible. There is such a constant, abundant flow of blessings into the life of the genuine student. How God blessed His chosen people (Israel), even though weak and fallen, when they gathered together "in the square" and gave attentive ears to Ezra as he (and his companions) "read from the Book of the Law of God, making it clear and giving the meaning so that the people could understand what was being read" (Nehemiah 8:1-8). There are so many blessings awaiting your effort. May we list seven?

1. These are words that *reveal* divine wisdom. This is the Book of God (1 Thessalonians 2:13). Do you want to know the nature of God? Read Acts 17:23-31; Romans 1:16-32; Hebrews 6:17,18. To know the person of Jesus Christ? Read Matthew 16:16; John 1:1-14; 20:30,31; Philippians 2:5-11; 2 Peter 1:16-18. Do you need to know more about the identity of the Holy Spirit? Read John 16:7-15; Romans 8:9-17, 26; 1 Corinthians 2:6-13; 12:3,4,11. Concerning the will of God? See Isaiah 55:6-9; John 6:39,40. For the love and grace of God, see John 3:16; Acts 20:24; Romans 5:8-11; Ephesians 2:4,5; 3:18,19; Hebrews 2:9; 1 John 2:1,2; 4:8-11. The standard of right and wrong is defined in Jeremiah 10:23; Proverbs 14:12; Micah 6:8; Ecclesiastes 12:13,14; Exodus 20:1-17; Matthew 22:36-40; James 1:27.

2. These are words that *save* the soul. Is there any greater blessing than this? If it is urgent for one to grasp the words of his physician in order to save the body from pain and disease and death, how much more imperative are God's words of salvation from eternal punishment — to the rich inheritance of everlasting life with God (Luke 1:76-79; John 5:39; 6:68; Acts 20:32; 1 Corinthians 1:21; 2 Timothy 3:15; James 1:21).

3. These are words that *instruct* the mind in all manner of righteousness. It is plain common sense to want to know what is good for oneself and to study in order to find out

(Acts 17:11). No situation nor condition of life is found without God's instruction on how one is to answer it — somewhere in Scripture the student should find just the right truth for his problem. Understand the Word so that you will know how to grow (2 Timothy 3:16,17) more godly (2 Peter 1:3) and righteous (Romans 6:17,18; 2 Corinthians 5:21).

4. These are words that *strengthen* the soul. Is there any one of us who at some time does not need comfort (1 Thessalonians 4:18; Isaiah 51:12; 2 Corinthians 1:3-5; Matthew 11:28), peace (Psalm 119:165), protection (1 Peter 5:7), strength (Psalm 27:1), hope and assurance (Romans 15:4; 2 Timothy 1:12)?

5. These are words that are *spiritual*. Less and less we need to speak the language of men and more and more we need to talk as God talks (Colossians 3:16) so that we shall be able to speak His language and understand our Creator (1 Corinthians 2:1-16).

6. These are words that are *profitable*. They work! They accomplish in us what God intended them to accomplish. That is why they were recorded for us (1 Corinthians 10:11; 1 Thessalonians 2:13; Hebrews 4:12).

7. Finally, these are words that *will last*. They are not temporary. They are not outdated (Matthew 24:35; 1 Peter 1:25). And this is even more significant when we understand that someday we shall all be judged by them (John 12:48).

See Bibliography for a list of tools.

Questions for Review

1. What is unique about the Bible as a book to understand?
2. What is the difference between reading and studying the Bible?
3. Name at least five reasons why people do not study the Bible.
4. Name at least twelve tools one needs to be a good student of the Bible.
5. When do you feel is the best time during the day to study your Bible? Why?
6. Describe the place where you prefer to study the Bible, and tell why you prefer it.
7. Name at least two systems you have used to study.

Assignments for Study

1. Have each person bring his study Bible to class.
2. Assign five students the task of bringing to class the five tools (concordance, Bible dictionary, maps or an atlas of Bible lands, a modern speech Bible, and a commentary) and explain how each should be used.

Topics for Discussion

1. Discuss the good and bad points of the study Bibles brought to class.
2. Name four sound study habits and tell how each should be developed.

CHAPTER THREE

Use Common Sense

"Therefore do not be foolish, but understand what the Lord's will is"
(Ephesians 5:17).

One of the most pathetic enemies of the Bible is the student who uses poor reasoning. The Bible is different from other books because it is divinely authored by God. This we have already studied. However, in other ways the Bible should be treated with logic and common sense as any ordinary, intelligent writing.

Of course, the issue of human reason can be overemphasized. It can actually become one's god. On the other hand, it can be tragically omitted altogether. What is the proper place of reason in the matter? By the powers of the mind we can (1) determine from evidence that the Bible is the Word of God, and then (2) employ these powers to understand it. The mind should never create religious truth, only picture it in its true focus.

What is good thinking? Thinking is difficult to explain. Basically, good thinking is the mental activity whereby one observes facts to see how they are related, grasps the total picture in its true light, and draws sound conclusions. We need to do this in everyday life. What makes us think the Bible is an exception? If we violate the principles of logic and common sense in politics, business, or any other field, are we

not likely to do the same with the Bible? Is it not then important that the student learn the art of common sense? What
good are all the tools mentioned in the preceding chapter if
this one proves to be deficient? Did you ever have the experience of building something, later to find that one of the most
important tools was inferior? What happened? Did it not
affect the entire project, in spite of the fact that all the other
tools were good?

Some people have had the false notion that even though
they are not good at practical reasoning on secular knowledge because they are inclined to be dreamy and imaginative,
they are thus more apt to be good Bible students. Nothing
could be further from the truth. The Bible declares again and
again that man can easily be deceived (Matthew 24:5;
1 Corinthians 3:18; 2 Peter 2:1-3; Ephesians 5:6; 2 Thessalonians 2:3).

The art of good reasoning is a natural qualification and
must be understood and developed. It can be done by taking
a little time to learn simple rules of logic, by self-observation,
and then by self-discipline. One must be humble and teachable. Such effort will prove most rewarding. Remember the
adage, "Don't be so busy sawing wood that you haven't time
to sharpen the saw." Good judgment can grow. Learning to
know and avoid the main hindrances to common sense will
greatly affect all the studies that follow in this book.

The Weaknesses of the Mind

This subject could occupy dozens of volumes, but our purpose is not to give an exhaustive study on logic. This is a field
all of its own. It is, however, our desire to expose those violations of common sense that contribute so frequently to our
misunderstanding the Bible. God's Word has been badly misused, abused, misunderstood, and misrepresented. Herein
we would like to present six of the most common and deadly
practices of poor thinking affecting our theme. And it would
be well to note that these often overlap each other, some-

times more than one weakness being present at a given time.

1. *Prejudice* — what is it? It is the common spirit of bias and partiality to which all mankind is subject, more or less. It is a general term and fittingly the first we should list. All the other weaknesses that follow are actually more specific phases of prejudice.

No one is completely free of prejudice. It is impossible for one to openly face every issue freely and fully without being partial to some degree. We have been too deeply involved in the ordinary feelings and influences of life. However, we can carefully study the nature of prejudices and make allowance for them, and so approach the Bible with a degree of objectivity. To be ideally unprejudiced one would have to be possessed with a pure desire to arrive at the full truth of Scripture without having a single preference or opinion or without being disturbed by any feeling of affection or dislike.

Why are we prejudiced? There are many reasons. We are too involved in personal experiences, inclined to have favorite ideas, eager to have lesser desires gratified and controlled by feelings. Look at our past experiences and early training. These things are hard to unlearn. Hold out a crumpled ten dollar bill and a shiny new quarter to a little child. Which will he usually take? He will choose the quarter, of course, because he does not know its real value. Instead he has had many experiences with brightly colored toys. Later on, by experience, he will learn better, simply because differences in value will become clearer. But think of how many prejudices, more subtle, he will always carry with him. You can see how your early ideas on religion, morals, and doctrine will affect your approach to the Bible.

Let us look at the influence of experiences and associations. A young man, away from home and fighting a war, is befriended by a Roman Catholic priest. How it colors his view of Catholic doctrine. Or take the case of a man who complained to the writer about his bitter experience with a church and a preacher. He had become so prejudiced that he could not be touched by the Scriptures.

To close this part, examine one more significant cause of prejudice — the effect of fear and feelings. This was illustrated so clearly by the lady who actually said in good faith, "I should go to the doctor and have a physical checkup, but I'm afraid he will find something wrong with me." There are many who have exactly the same prejudice toward the Bible.

2. *Preconceived Opinion.* This comes from the practice of supposing something exists or assuming something is true without sufficient study or proof. Often the mind is made up before the Bible facts are seen. This is a dangerous practice. It has given rise to many false ideas. It corrupts the attitude of the Bible student. It causes some to bring their ideas to the Scriptures for approval, not for testing. It plays up the passages that seem to defend the opinion and plays down any that contradict it.

We are reminded of a practice that was all too common during Civil War days. Both the Northerner and the Southerner flew to the Scriptures to defend and support opposite opinions on slavery. However, we are to go to the Bible to *obtain* our doctrine, not to *sustain* it. People who look to the Bible for proof of their opinions fail to be interpreters of the Word. Actually they expect the Bible to become a mirror of their own views.

Consider the Jews in Jesus' day. They had developed their own opinions as to what the Messiah was to do and be. When Jesus declared himself to be the Messiah, they ran to the Scriptures, not to learn, but only to substantiate what they had felt about Jesus all along. Later Paul declared that they refused to see this truth because "their minds were made dull, for to this day the same veil remains when the old covenant is read. It has not been removed, because only in Christ is it taken away" (2 Corinthians 3:14).

This habit grows progressively worse in many people. The stronger the assumption, the more one fights the truth. A case in point is the person who declares he cannot remember names. The more he assumes this is true, the more forgetful he becomes. Even so, the more common these preconceived ideas of Scripture become, the more one actually will fight the plain facts of the Bible. Preconceived ideas are very apt to run wild in the field of prophecy and in regard to personal wishes and feelings. This leads to the next violation.

3. *Wishful Thinking.* Some persons wish so strongly that something be true that they come to believe firmly that it is true. We all have our desires, our wants, and our loves. We have our feelings. How often does some thought we hold prove to be nothing more than a reflection of what we really love and want? But wishing a thing were true, and even repeating it over and over, does not make it true.

An example is the common experience of a person losing a loved one in death. Let us say the deceased had some remarkable virtue or accomplishment to his credit. And yet this person had never taken Jesus as his Savior. Memories are tender and precious, love is strong, and hope for future reward and reunion is overpowering. Is not one greatly tempted to believe what he wants to believe? Is it not easy to create a doctrine of salvation for this loved one, even though the Scripture would give no such hope?

Another form of this weakness is called "rationalizing." This is nothing more than searching for apparently logical reasons for doing what we want to do, or intend to do. The best examples of this can be found in the dozens of excuses people give for not attending church. Most of them are vain efforts to make their reasons for doing things other than attending services sound plausible.

This borders on dishonesty. Nothing is more deadly to the student than being a dishonest searcher for truth. All the rules of Bible interpretation fall before the dishonest heart. They are helpless when faced by one who desires to do as he wishes and then to be covered by an array of excuses.

4. *Generalization.* This is the fallacy of drawing sweeping conclusions from particular instances. This is being done

every day. For example, a student fails to study his lesson and is surprised by a test the following day. This happens two or three times and he complains, "Every time I don't study, the teacher gives a test." Or how often have you heard people say, "Every time I wash the car it rains," or "The church is full of hypocrites," or "Preachers' kids usually turn out bad." These are all cases of making unwarranted sweeping conclusions from specific cases.

For example, take the case of a man who quotes a couple of isolated verses from the Bible: "Use a little wine because of your stomach" (1 Timothy 5:23) and "Every man . . . is temperate in all things" (1 Corinthians 9:25, King James Version). Then, disregarding the context and everything else written on the subject, he makes a sweeping conclusion and boldly declares his personal doctrine on the subject of drinking. To caption it off with finality he usually will add, "And my uncle drank whiskey every day of his life and lived to be ninety-six."

We can see the danger of oversimplifying issues in the Bible that have many facets of truth and conditions to consider. It is more dangerous to draw such wide conclusions from single passages of Scripture. But jumping at conclusions seems to be one of man's most common exercises. We must remember that many Bible issues are not simply "black and white." Often there are more than two sides. However, when all the facts have been observed and weighed, then it is perfectly justifiable to generalize.

5. *Appeals to Human Authority.* This is the practice of "throwing around the weight" of big names or authorities, regardless of truthfulness and condition, in order to defend a point, usually biased. This is not to depreciate scholarship nor belittle true authority. You have heard people defend themselves with the magic words, "Science says . . ." Or, in religion, how often one feels justified in his opinion by saying, "My preacher says so" or "That's what my church teaches."

There are several such authorities people use. It may be

great men, church creeds, human tradition, or books and sayings. Some people think that merely to mention a scholar's name is enough to freeze all further thought and investigation. This should not be so. True scholarship never closes the door so dogmatically. It carries weight, but is never final. Only God is final in authority.

Then some feel that there is great weight in the clever, trite sayings of man. You have heard them, such as "The fatherhood of God and the brotherhood of man," or "No man who lives morally right can be doctrinally wrong." These are easily spoken and they make good conversation, but whether they are the truth of God as revealed in Scripture is another question. Beware of them, especially when they become guides to your Bible study. All preachers have witnessed the death of one who has committed about every sin in the Bible, only to hear someone murmur with deep conviction, "But he was really good at heart."

Another kind of "authoritarian" appeal is the use of figures. Statistics, improperly used and related, can prove most anything. Like the expert who revealed his findings by stating that all Harvard graduates (male) for a given period of time averaged 2.6 children each during his married life, while Radcliffe graduates (female) for the same period averaged 2.3 children each. This proves that men have more children than women. How foolish! Yet we must be careful about applying the same principle to Bible study. Some people feel that a doctrine may be proved by quoting dozens of passages in its defense. They depend on the number of passages quoted alone, not on their correct meaning and application.

One argument that some have used in the past against the doctrine of the virgin birth of Jesus is that two of the Gospel writings and all of Paul's letters fail to literally teach it. Therefore, they conclude that the silence of so many New Testament books on such an important matter proves that it must not be true. However, Matthew and Luke both clearly teach that Jesus was virgin-born. How many times does God have to say something to make it true?

6. *Appeals to the Popular.* This is the exceedingly strong motive better known as "getting along with the crowd." Who wants to differ with popular opinion? How hard it is to fight the prejudices of our age! It is very easy to find a crowd who will agree with your prejudices.

All of us are influenced in part by what others think, but sometimes we are controlled too much by this force. You have heard people attempt to pry others loose with the magic words, "They say . . ." This is a challenge to people to discard independent thinking and think like the masses and talk like "all the scholars." We laugh when the television announcer, dressed in a white coat, gives a clinical demonstration and urges us to "do as millions do, buy 'Germ-off' soap." Of course, the next time we visit the store we buy it.

The sad part is that we practice this same weakness in our Bible study. What are some of the most popular cries that affect our study? "It doesn't make a difference what we believe, just so we are sincere." "A person can't be all bad; there is good in all people and churches." "There are so many churches, but they are all headed for the same place." Few people have any idea how much of an influence the simple philosophy, "a million people can't be wrong," has on our understanding the Bible. Look how many in the world five hundred years ago believed the world was flat — a great number did.

Don't ever be afraid to stand alone. Remember the words of Henry Clay, "I would rather be right than president." Sir William Drummond once said, "He who will not reason is a bigot; he who cannot is a fool; and he who dares not is a slave." Have an obsession to understand God's truth regardless of popular opinion. What is popular today may be outmoded tomorrow. Stand for the eternal truths that never change.

Questions for Review

1. What is the twofold function of the mind in studying the Bible?
2. Why is good thinking important?
3. Name the six violations of common sense and define each.

Assignments for Study

Have various members of the class consider one of the six weaknesses in reasoning, and name at least one Bible example for each (other than those cases mentioned in the chapter), showing how misunderstanding is produced by such fallacies.

Topics for Discussion

In order to show the folly of generalizing in regard to the use of only a few passages of Scripture, look up the following fifteen verses: Matthew 1:21; Acts 2:40; 3:19; 16:31; Romans 3:23,24; 5:10; 8:24; 10:9,13; 1 Corinthians 15:1,2; Ephesians 1:7; 1 Timothy 4:10; James 1:21; 2:24; 1 Peter 3:20,21; Revelation 2:10. Notice that each reveals something that saves a person from sin. Discuss how all of these different things contribute to a person's salvation and why each should be included in drawing a final conclusion on the subject.

CHAPTER FOUR

Ten Essential Attitudes

"They are darkened in their understanding . . .
due to the hardening of their hearts"
(Ephesians 4:18).

Often you have heard people thank God for a "free country" and a "free Bible" (an expression from the Reformation,
before which the Bible was not accessible to the common
man). This is indeed a blessing. Nevertheless, this means but
one thing — we live in a land and at a time when God's Word
is completely available. We are at liberty to know and understand it. Yet compared with other writings, the Bible is one
of the most abused, misused, misrepresented, and misunderstood books in the world. This fact certainly curbs the free-
dom of the Bible. In many different ways the revealed truth
is enslaved, so that it might as well be chained in a dungeon
or read under threat of imprisonment. The sad thing is that
man continually enslaves the Bible through the many weaknesses expressed in this study.

One of the most prevalent causes of misunderstanding the
Bible is that the student fails to approach the Bible with the
right attitude. In this way, God's method of teaching him the
truth is thwarted from the very beginning. This is the problem Jesus faced as He began His ministry among men. After
His famous parable of the sower, spoken before the multi-

tudes, the disciples asked why He had used this method. The reply of Jesus indicated that the parable method was used so that only those who possessed the wholesome, willing attitude to know and understand what He said would actually understand it. Those whose attitudes were wrong in any way would see, but not perceive, and hear, but not understand (Read Matthew 13:1-23). Is this not the reason why many people of Jesus' own nation never understood God's great truth as revealed by His Son in person?

It is highly important that we prepare ourselves with the proper attitudes as we approach the Bible for study. Following are ten essentials in this study.

Be Willing to Work

The spirit of work we name first. There is no other attitude nor activity that will take its place. You must work for what you get, you must sow for what you reap. We said before that this is true of any worthwhile endeavor of life. Those who seek any branch of knowledge must pursue it with vigor and labor. Work little or toil with little zeal and the results will be little. "Getting something for nothing" is more than a common expression; it is a delusion. Bible knowledge is no different.

Back in the beginning when man sinned, God cursed the ground and said, "By the sweat of your brow you will eat your food" (Genesis 3:19). That basic principle, which applies to physical bread, is equally true of spiritual bread. If you want to partake of God's truth, you will have to work for it. Bible study must become a job, not just a hobby; a habit, not just an impulse; an obsession, not just a whim.

With all Timothy's advantages of family background and training, it was necessary for Paul to give the commandment, "Do your best to present yourself to God as one approved, a workman who does not need to be ashamed, and who correctly handles the word of truth" (2 Timothy 2:15). Too many fail to understand the Bible because they are unwilling to make the effort. Contrary to this, the Bereans were praised because they were willing to search the Scriptures (Acts 17:11,12).

Trust the Word of God

Next, we must have complete trust in the Word. The effective reader must study the Bible, never wavering in his faith that it is the Word of God. Doubts will surely weaken the understanding. Unbelief will "blind the mind" (2 Corinthians 4:3,4).

One must be humble and teachable as a little child. There must be complete trust. He who mistrusts will never be in the frame of mind to understand much of what God says. He may know many things regarding the Scripture, but he will understand relatively little. We cannot comprehend the great truth of the Lord, if we accept the Bible as only fiction or unreliable history. "And we also thank God continually because, when you received the word of God, which you heard from us, you accepted it not as the word of men, but as it actually is, the word of God, which is at work in you who believe" (1 Thessalonians 2:13). Let us say with the psalmist, "I trust in your word" (Psalm 119:42).

Show Reverence for the Word

The spirit of reverence for the Word should follow, in view of this complete trust. It must be held with the highest respect, regarded as more necessary than anything else in life (Job 23:12; Luke 4:4). It is the full and final will of God for man, the standard of authority in all matters of morals, and therefore it must be free from all human tamperings (Deuteronomy 12:32; Revelation 22:18,19).

Irreverence is a mark of our times. Man is as apt to take the Word of God in vain as he is to take the name of God in vain. There can be such an absence of respect for the things of God.

Reverence is "a respectful, submissive disposition of mind,

arising from affection and esteem, from a sense of superiority in the person reverenced."[1] Reverence involves the feeling of awe, deep veneration, and fear because God is present. It is an inward attitude outwardly manifested by respect, sobriety, and rapt attention. Reverence is a Christian virtue (Hebrews 12:28) that demands effort. This self-discipline of mind and body should be applied whenever the Word of God is studied.

It would be well for us to go back and restudy the occasion when God gave the law to Israel from Mount Sinai, and observe how the people fell back in fear and consternation as God solemnly warned all not even to touch the mountain. God was speaking! To have profound respect for the Bible is not to worship a book, but to reverence the Lord God who gave it.

Expect Delight

To delight in the Word, to thoroughly enjoy its study, is an attitude that should do much to produce understanding. Do you "rejoice at His word" (Psalm 119:162)? Can it be said that your "delight is in the law of the Lord" (Psalm 1:2)?

Avoid making Bible study such a dutiful task and such miserable drudgery. Enjoy it! Don't think the Bible is dry inside just because yours is dusty on the outside. It can and should become a real pleasure. It can be alive and delightful if you let it. We stated that it would be work; nevertheless, it can be a most satisfying ad thrilling task. The Bible has all the elements to bring the joys of God to your soul. Surely He knows best how to impart real happiness to His own creatures.

Love the Word

Your reverence and joy in the Bible should thus blend

---

[1]*The Popular and Critical Bible Encyclopedia* (Chicago: The Howard-Severance Company, 1907), III, 1469.

together to produce in you a genuine love for the Word. Actually, in all walks of life we pursue that which we love. No one has to be prodded to do what he really loves. We are willing to even expend ourselves for those worthy objects of our love. What is more worthy, more lovable, than the Word of our Lord? "O how love I your law! I meditate on it all day long" (Psalm 119:97; see also verses 113, 159, 167).

It is natural that we earnestly seek to know and embrace the Scriptures that we love. In so doing, we hasten to understand and protect the Word. This leads to the sixth essential attitude.

Desire to Understand the Word

We must desire to understand the truth, but this is most difficult! If we love self more than we love God, then we shall be guilty of self-satisfaction and self-conceit. Here are two of the most common reasons why man is unwilling to understand the Bible. This is the way a selfish young man often loves a young lady. He loves her for only what pleasure she brings to him — thus really loving himself, not her. We must not allow our determination to seek the truth deteriorate into the plight expressed in the words, "the truth as I see it."

Let us realize what it means to have the desire to be a completely honest inquirer into the truth. Are you willing to yield to the Bible, wherever it leads? Are you able to endure all truth, no matter how uncomfortable? Are you willing to arrive at the truth, disregarding your own opinion, emotion, desire, or hope? Are you willing to search each new fact without any fear of what you might find? Are you willing to see both sides of any issue? Are you willing to study what you dislike as well as what you like? Are you willing, at all costs, to avoid the mental errors listed in the last chapter? If you are unwilling, then your understanding of the Word will be greatly impaired, no matter how much you study it.

The Bible is divine truth (John 17:17). It is to be desired above all that is human. "Blessed are those who hunger and thirst for righteousness, for they will be filled" (Matthew 5:6). Lord Bacon once prayed for understanding "that by our minds thoroughly cleansed and purged from fancy and vanities, and yet subject and perfectly given up to the Divine oracles" one would truly be a child of faith. "The law of the Lord is perfect, reviving the soul. The statutes of the Lord are trustworthy, making wise the simple. . . . They are more precious than gold, than much fine gold" (Psalm 19:7,10).

Shun Perversions of the Word

If one is to desire the truth, one will be equally as zealous to shun error. The two, positive and negative, go hand in hand. As we stand before God with His Word in our hands, we have everything to learn and nothing to teach. How repugnant, then, when any false doctrine intervenes to spoil the pure truth. It should be identified and avoided or discarded as false. This is what the Scriptures teach over and over again. Read 2 Timothy 3 and note how Paul describes those who are "always learning but never able to acknowledge the truth" (2 Timothy 3:7). Trace God's warnings in the following passages:

"many . . . peddle the word of God for profit" (2 Corinthians 2:17)

"some people . . . are trying to pervert the gospel" (Galatians 1:6-8)

"cunning and craftiness of men in their deceitful scheming" (Ephesians 4:14)

"so that no one may deceive you by fine-sounding arguments" (Colossians 2:4)

"See to it that no one takes you captive through hollow and deceptive philosophy, which depends on human tradition" (Colossians 2:8)

"does not agree to the sound instruction . . . . He has an unhealthy interest in controversies and quarrels about words that result in envy, strife, malicious talk, evil suspicions and constant friction" (1 Timothy 6:3-5) "quarreling about words; . . . of no value, . . . godless chatter" (2 Timothy 2:14,16)

"teaching things they ought not to teach" (Titus 1:11)

"They will secretly introduce destructive heresies . . . . these teachers will exploit you with stories they have made up" (2 Peter 2:1-3)

"Anyone who runs ahead and does not continue in the teaching of Christ does not have God" (2 John 9).

Remember, the Lord will permit you to accept and believe a lie if you want to. If man desires error more than truth, he will find it, and the result is damnation (2 Thessalonians 2:10-12).

The honest student must rise above every tendency to please himself or the world, and strive to possess the twofold desire to know truth and avoid error, at all costs.

Undergird Study With Prayer

Before ever beginning to expend such effort and maintaining such attitudes, one should turn and ask the Lord for help through prayer. The Lord will teach us much and help us to learn, but we need not expect Him to do for us what we ought to do for ourselves. The prayers of a lazy, halfhearted, grumbling student cannot rise very high.

Is not prayer a practice more than an attitude? It is both, as shown in more than one of the ten points cited. A prayerful attitude is so vital, and God has promised to respond to such pleadings. "If any of you lacks wisdom, he should ask God, who gives generously to all without finding fault, and it will be given to him" (James 1:5). Let the spirit of prayer pervade all your efforts to understand the Bible.

Have a Spirit of Expectancy

In view of all that has been said thus far, is it not reasonable that the spirit of expectancy must follow? Does not the student have the right to expect to understand this Book?

Many are amazed, frightened or overwhelmed by the bigness of the Bible; yet, it can be read completely through in one hundred hours, and a rapid reader might read it in sixty hours. Yes, to some it is a big, mysterious, unfathomable something, a complicated collection of deep, religious doctrines. Some consider it to be a strange writing to be worshiped and not used, a mystery to be understood only by a favored few, or a handbook of proof texts for sectarian groups.

But when we start to study the Bible, we ought to expect to understand it. Our understanding of a particular passage might not be perfect, but we must remember that God revealed His will to us in order that we may understand it. It is to be "read to all the brothers" (1 Thessalonians 5:27), so that when it is read, "the Lord will give you insight into all this" (2 Timothy 2:7). The very purpose is that the reader may understand the knowledge of God (Ephesians 3:3,4), the knowledge that makes "you wise for salvation" and brings Christian maturity (2 Timothy 3:14-17).

Oftentimes you will be tempted to stop trying to understand the Bible, or be disturbed over specific passages that you do not fully understand. Nevertheless, you can and will understand most of it. God promised it; so expect it (2 Corinthians 1:13,14).

Desire to Be Obedient

Finally, as the understanding grows, be sure and have a genuine desire to obey the Word. A mere curiosity about the Bible or an academic interest in it is not enough. God's word demands a greater desire — a desire to apply the holy truth, to live the way the Creator intended one to live. Let each Bible student say, "Teach me, O LORD, to follow your decrees; then I will keep them to the end. Give me understanding, and I will keep your law and obey it with all my heart" (Psalm 119:33,34).

This brings us to the same closing point mentioned in the first chapter. Disobedience to the Word as it is received will only hinder or stop the progress of further understanding. The Word of God is food for the soul. If the simple food (milk) is refused, then the solid food will be withheld because it cannot be assimilated. Read 1 Corinthians 3:1-4; Hebrews 5:12-14.

In conclusion, may it be clear that unless the attitude of the student is right, all the methods and rules in the world will avail very little. But with the right spirit of mind and heart, one may grow in the grace and knowledge of our Lord.

Questions for Review

1. Why is one's attitude in Bible study so important?
2. Why did Jesus often teach in parables?
3. Why is the spirit of work important?
4. What does the word "reverence" mean? How would you apply this to Bible study?
5. Why are "self-satisfaction" and "self-conceit" so detrimental to understanding the Bible?
6. Why is it important to "shun error" as well as to "desire the truth"?
7. What must one do before one can properly pray for understanding?
8. What should be your attitude when you come to a passage which you cannot understand?

Assignments for Study

1. Memorize the ten correct attitudes for the Bible student.
2. Explain briefly each one.

Topics for Discussion

1. List some bad attitudes that hinder one's understanding of the Bible. Tell why in each case.
2. Consider at least six good questions that would test one's desire to know the truth. Then call for practical examples in life that demonstrate these points.

CHAPTER FIVE

Methods of Interpretation

"His letters contain some things that are hard to understand,
which ignorant and unstable people distort,
as they do the other Scriptures, to their own destruction"
(2 Peter 3:16).

We have already touched on a number of reasons why people fail to understand the Bible. Sometimes the obvious reason is that persons use faulty tools, or lack tools altogether. Then again, it may be a deficiency in attitude. If one has little desire to know the truth, is afraid of the truth, or has no ambition to work for an understanding, either ignorance or misunderstanding will result. No method or rule can win out against a dishonest or unwilling heart. Look at the issue of pride alone. We shall never fully see how much this sin affects our lack of understanding the Bible. It often creeps into our thinking in many different ways, and then deceives us in its very operation (Romans 12:3; 1 Corinthians 3:18; 10:12; Galatians 6:3). Also, we considered how important it is to be guided by all the rules of common sense, so that the powers of reason would be at their best.

Is this not true of any study? Consider how these same things enter the picture as one tries to master such common subjects as learning to drive an automobile, understanding a course in current history, or becoming skilled in the art of farming.

Look at the abuses we have inflicted upon the Bible. We have treated it as a mystical charm. The mere possession of it or carrying it on the person replaces the use of it. Sometimes we treat it as a "box of sweets," picking out what we like and leaving what we don't like; and then we are tempted to overeat on those few chosen pieces. Sometimes we treat the Bible as some kind of a smorgasbord, sampling a little here and there at random, as though such indiscriminate sampling will provide us with a well-rounded spiritual diet. Others dutifully accept the Bible as some kind of a reading rosary — so many verses are covered each day enabling God to mark the "good credit" side of the ledger in heaven.

We now approach the next issue at hand, the *method* to be employed in order to study the Bible with understanding. This has one of the most subtle of all influences on our understanding, or lack of it.

The Need for a Method

Some have chosen no particular method of studying the Bible, nor see any need for such a choice, because they feel it is a strange or mystically different book. They are marked by the practice of flipping open the Bible, spearing a verse at random and fully expecting God to send a flash of truth as a panacea for the problem being faced at the time. They may feel that such a holy book can be known only by some supernatural interpretation or authorized interpreter. Others treat the Bible as one big riddle, with one person's opinion about it being just as good as another's. No other book in the world is treated this way. Is it any wonder that honest, intelligent readers of an intelligible revelation are so confused today? Efficient or practical ways of study have been thrown to the wind or replaced by ways that reveal an extremely superstitious people at work in an enlightened age.

1. The Bible is a *normal message*, even though God is its author in a very special sense. He has simply addressed man as he is — in his natural state. Though it is the divine message

from God, nevertheless, it is still a message. Therefore it ought to be treated as such — by a normal, intelligent approach.

God has given many wonderful faculties, the highest of which is human reason. It is quite natural, then, to expect God to appeal to man's reason when He reaches down to communicate with him. In no way does this discredit the work of the Holy Spirit. He was sent to reveal divine truth. However, He does it through the Word (Ephesians 6:17; 1 Peter 1:22-25).

The Bible should be interpreted in the same manner as any other book. As John Allen Hudson quotes J.S. Lamar as saying,

> To adopt any other course, or to apply any other rules, would necessarily divest the sacred writings of every attribute that belongs to the idea of revelation. It must never be forgotten in pursuing the Bible, that in the structure of sentences, in figures of speech, in the arrangement and use of words, it differs not at all from all other writings, and must, therefore, be understood and interpreted as they are.[1]

2. This means that there is *original thought* in the message. This is always true in human communications. For example, a young person arrives home from school. There on the kitchen table is a note addressed to him and written by his mother. Immediately he realizes that she had a thought to convey from her mind to his. He wants to know what it was.

Don't you want to know the thoughts of God that prompted their being recorded?

3. Next, we believe that God has *revealed* that thought to man through Scriptures. The word "reveal" means, "To take off the cover, to disclose," as one would take that which was hidden and throw light on it so that it becomes clearly exposed. So the Bible is the thoughts of God that He saw fit

---

[1]*How to Read the Bible* (Fort Worth, TX: The Manney Company, 1958), p. 17.

to make open and clear to man (Romans 16:25,26; Ephesians 3:1-5; Colossians 1:25,26). If it requires some special key to understand, then it would not be an adequate revelation. The Bible does not create truth, it only exposes it so man can see it.

4. This message is written in ordinary *human language* — the language that God knew man would understand. In this way, God is doing all He can to help us understand what He means by what He says. We should then expect to accept the normal meanings of language. If God has adopted the word method of communicating with us, we should be eager to be regulated by all the accepted laws of word communication.

5. Thus, the Word of God must be *interpreted*, but correctly so. To interpret means "to explain or tell the meaning of." This meaning must be exactly what God intended it to be — that original thought as God couched it in human language. This must be the only meaning of the word "interpretation." The Bible student may not understand why God said it; he is only expected to understand what God said. To get into one's mind the fullness of thought that God originated and intended man to know is the full duty of the Bible interpreter.

6. The Bible must *never be misinterpreted*. If this is true of human-to-human communications, how much more important in divine-to-human communication!

The interpreter never has the right to inject his own opinions into that which God has revealed. This is why Peter wrote, "Above all, you must understand that no prophecy of Scripture came about by the prophet's own interpretation. For prophecy never had its origin in the will of man, but men spoke from God as they were carried along by the Holy Spirit" (2 Peter 1:20,21). We never have the right to overread the Bible (put more into the written words), nor do we have the right to underread it (put less into the words than God intended). The practice of interpreting must never deteriorate into personal guessing.

7. Finally, we have to apply the same *scientific principles* to interpreting the Bible that we use in our normal, intelligent communications with man. We must use an orderly procedure, a sensible way of investigating, a systematic plan to study the Bible. This is what we mean by method. If our method is not correct, then rules will accomplish little.

A poor system has produced many misunderstandings of the Bible, and when such methods are consistently used, the errors multiply. J.R. Stroop writes, "The more strongly one becomes attached to error, the more blinded he is to truth and the less capable of judging between truth and error, and the more helpless and the more hopeless his case becomes."[2]

Harmful Methods

Over the past centuries there have developed at least seven different methods of interpreting the Bible. These are being used today — although the great multitude of readers are not aware that they are using one or more of these methods. It is little wonder that the end results are sometimes so varied and contradictory. This is one of the reasons why people come up with so many different answers, all the while using the same Bible. This is why so many false doctrines are born and kept alive.

Let us identify and define these approaches which are so harmful. Let us then see to it that we refrain from such methods.

1. *Mystic Method.* One of the oldest avenues of approach to understanding the real meaning of Scripture is the "mystic." This comes from an old heathen idea that only certain persons are "in tune" with God and can get the real meaning out of the written word. One who uses this method believes that behind the recorded word (literal), there is a mystical meaning — and the latter is the real truth of God and the spiritual

---

[2]*Why Do People Not See the Bible Alike?* (Nashville: David Lipscomb College, 1949), p. 135.

meaning that one should desire. One is then led to believe that the literal word of the Bible is inferior, even useless or dangerous, and must be discarded if unacceptable.

The contradiction here is that one is urged to read the Bible in order to draw out the real spiritual meaning, but to discard the literal meaning as the reader learns better. One is said to be throwing away the outer shell after having reached the truth. This method becomes evident today in the common expression, "the letter and the spirit," when actually the Bible uses of this expression have nothing to do with this idea at all. The evil result of this theory has been indifference, and even contempt for the written Word of God. It teaches that the real truth is often altogether different from that which is obviously said. "*If the Bible does not mean what it says*, there is no way by which we can know what it does mean."[3] Then too, such an approach gives birth to many doctrines foreign to Scripture.

2. *Allegorical Method.* This is much like the first, only more extreme in degree. The word means to teach something by the use of symbols and figures of speech. In following this method, the reader treats the entire Bible as one big riddle. Then each one has the right to draw out of the various passages the lesson he feels is true for him. Everyone has equal privilege to do so.

There is a vast difference between a revelation and a riddle.

3. *Superstitious Method.* Here we find a method rich in emotion and poor in reason. As Paul said, "They are zealous for God, but their zeal is not based on knowledge" (Romans 10:2).

Here the reader becomes almost a "book idolater" digging for all manner of hidden meanings. This is done by a passionate working over thoughts, numbers, items, etc., in the Bible and combining them so they form strange conclusions and

---

[3]D.R. Dungan, *Hermeneutics* (Cincinnati: Standard Publishing), p. 60.

odd arrangements. It plays up incidental details into weird items of importance. It forces comparisons and contrasts. It thrives on originality rather than accuracy. It confuses all the orderly arrangements and divisions naturally found in the Bible.

4. *Ecclesiastical Method.* Here is the method that has grown throughout the ages and is used often by people today. The word "ecclesiastic" pertains to the organized church — its authoritative doctrine and practice.

One who uses this method looks not to God nor to himself for understanding of the Bible, but to the final authority of his church. This means that the church leader or creed is the only true interpreter of what the Bible means, and such decrees are final. Every part of the Bible is understood only as it is in harmony with such authoritative explanations.

From this we must not draw the conclusion that all church scholars and writings are worthless. This is the other extreme. All that we are saying is that no church authority must be considered as the final, infallible interpreter of Scripture, regardless of what is thoroughly and honestly studied.

5. *Dogmatic Method.* Next we consider a method all too common and effective today. It is simply this: one assumes a certain doctrine is true, then he defends it by showing, from Scripture, he can prove it is true. This is never difficult to do. One can find most anything in the Bible if one wants to find it. It is called "proof-texting." This becomes very subtle, because all of us desire to give "chapter and verse" for what we believe.

To put it briefly, this method is used when one goes to the Bible to sustain his doctrine, not to obtain it.

6. *Rational Method.* The word "rational" refers to reason, and this is the method that exaggerates the position of reason. It ceases to treat reason as a tool, and makes it the supreme authority in all judgments of Scriptural truth.

The rationalist, or modernist, approaches the Bible and accepts all that is written, as long as it does not contradict what his own reason says is possible and feasible. The unreasonable parts are discarded and all passages are interpreted so as never to violate human reason. For example, he cuts out a miracle because it is not reasonable to experience, and he keeps what is left.

The great weakness here is that God's wisdom can never penetrate man's thinking. Man actually writes his own scripture as he reasons it out, using the Bible as an aid.

7. *Literal Method.* As a reactionary move against the rational method, some people are driven to the extreme of making every part of the Bible literal. They actually force the Bible to be literal at a point where obviously it is symbolic. Or they may quote all passages with equal weight as God's truth. This sometimes leads to putting a quotation of an uninspired man or of the devil himself on a par with the words of an inspired man. Sometimes people become fanatics by seeing things out of proportion, distorting incidental details, and misapplying passage after passage.

This is but to use the Bible for the mere sake of using it, but actually it is sheer misrepresentation.

The Inductive Method

Enough of the negative; let us now turn to the positive approach. After all, these seven methods are actually extremes. If we avoid these extremes and approach the Scriptures sanely, we shall be following the method of "induction."

Actually, the method one uses to approach the Bible will be determined by what he believes the Bible to be. In view of what has been said of the Word in previous lessons, it follows that we must let the Bible speak for itself as God's revelation.

The word "induction" means to reason by noting particular facts and instances, and from them drawing general conclusions. Let us permit God to give us the facts, and all the facts, exactly as He intended them through human language. Then let us draw those conclusions that are necessarily or reasonably implied. This is the only way that the Bible can possibly speak for itself.

God reveals himself to man through two important avenues. The first avenue we call natural or general revelation (the world about us, natural science) and the second we call special revelation (Bible). For centuries man has been using the inductive method in unlocking the mysteries of nature. After drawing out all the facts by scientific observation and tabulation he is ready to make sound scientific conclusions. Why shouldn't we do the same with God's Word? Both revelations were addressed to the same creatures.

Years ago, when P.S. Fall first heard Alexander Campbell preach, he said,

> It was seen at once that it was the duty of the speaker and the privilege of the hearer to ascertain simply *what the divine Word says, and why it is said.* We had been accustomed to make the Scriptures a book of text-proofs of our doctrines. We now saw that we had everything to learn but *nothing to prove* in using God's word. On the former plan we knew as much when we came to the Bible as when we left it. . . . Upon the new plan we had use for every word the Holy Spirit had spoken. We supposed ourselves to know nothing when we approached the sacred books, and were to be mere listeners and thereby learners.[4]

---

[4]Robert Richardson, *Memoirs of Alexander Campbell* (Cincinnati: Standard Publishing), II, 121.

Questions for Review

1. How has the Bible been abused in study?
2. Why is the method of study important?
3. What is meant by saying the Bible is a "normal message"?
4. What does the word "reveal" mean?
5. What should the word "interpret" mean?
6. What does it mean to "overread" and "underread" the message of the Bible?
7. What is meant by "method" of study?
8. Name the seven harmful methods mentioned and give their meanings, each in a brief sentence.
9. What does "induction" mean, as a study method?

Assignments for Study

1. Take the subject of "Conversion to Christ" and show how any of the harmful methods of studying this subject would produce misunderstanding. Point out the errors and weaknesses.
2. Next, using the same subject, show how the inductive method would lead to a correct understanding of it.

Topic for Discussion

Discuss the points where an inductive study of nature is similar to the same method of study of the Bible.

CHAPTER SIX

Rules of Interpretation

"Do your best to present yourself to God as one approved, a workman who does not need to be ashamed and who correctly handles the word of truth"
(2 Timothy 2:15).

The Bible is not a book of dull philosophies, miscellaneous sayings, or mystifying abstractions. It is alive! It is a message told in colorful human language, made clear, vivid, and true to life by examples, teachings, and history.

No two Bible students are exactly alike mentally — just as no two people have identical physical features. There are peculiarities, variations in powers of logic, memory, strength, weakness, etc. So, in the wake of a common sense *method* of approaching the Word, there must also be employed common sense *rules* to discipline the inquiring mind.

Quoting from Professor Seth Wilson,

> One can interpret well without formal study of any set of rules, but cannot interpret accurately at all without following (perhaps unconsciously) certain principles which are based upon the nature of the mind and of truth, and are inherent in the very structure of language.
>
> Such rules, of course, have no authority. No one is bound to accept any rule of hermeneutics [science of interpretation] unless it is found to be true to the facts and to be productive of correct results. . . .
>
> . . . They are truly scientific in that they are descriptive,

discovered, inductive, and without any authority except the accuracy with which they fit further experience. They are carefully stated descriptions of the way men regularly think and read when they get the meaning intended in any writing. They were not invented, but were discovered by observation of many experiences and are derived from analysis of many instances until a general statement could be made of what was regularly or always observed in cases of correct interpretation.[1]

These are not some special rules belonging only to Bible study. They are identical to the rules that we ordinarily employ in our daily interchange of thoughts between any two rational persons. Applied to Bible study, rules are nothing more than a means of disciplining the mind by which we allow the Bible to mean what it must mean, not what we want it to mean. Is there any subject not governed by common sense rules?

This plays a vital role in understanding the Bible. Rules do not necessarily make a good interpreter, just as rules do not necessarily make a boy a good ballplayer. However, it is a poor interpreter or a poor ballplayer who observes no rules. But it is essential to employ correct rules, for incorrect rules will produce incorrect understanding of the Bible. Rules that violate common sense or pure motives are false doctrines in themselves.

This is a science — a science of common sense. It has advanced much during the past four centuries. Like any science, it should be continually observed, tested, and used to seek new truth. God's Word always waits for man to use an ever-growing means to see fully all that is intended. Let us identify, learn, and use these rules. We name fifteen — the last four of which comprise the remaining lessons of this book.

---

[1]Seth Wilson, "Understanding God's Word," (Joplin, MO: Ozark Christian College, n.d.), p. 6.

The Rules

1. *Every passage has only one meaning.* Ordinarily a passage of Scripture has only one meaning. In any letter, discourse, book, or conversation in ordinary communication this is true, unless the author is seeking to mislead or confuse the reader, or conceal ignorance. We expect a writer to mean what he says, no more and no less.

When God commands a person to "pray without ceasing," states the fact that Jesus "arose from the grave," gives a warning against "hell" and the promise of "heaven," and tells the story of the "prodigal son," He is not giving riddles with variant meanings, but a single flow of thought for us to grasp. This is why the Bible tells us to ". . . agree with one another so that there may be no divisions among you and that you may be perfectly united in mind and thought" (1 Corinthians 1:10).

There are exceptions to this rule that in no way contradict it. Sometimes a prophecy was given that had an immediate meaning as well as a remote meaning — more than one fulfillment. The earlier served as a pledge for the latter.

In Psalm 16:10, David seems to speak of himself in a time of danger when he says, "because you will not abandon me to the grave, nor will you let your Holy One see decay." David trusts God to deliver him from the hands of his enemies. However, in Acts 2:27 the apostle Peter reveals that David spoke of the resurrection of Christ. Thus, David prophesied truth of the coming Messiah through the same words that held personal significance for his own day.

2. *The most simple and obvious meaning of any passage is usually the correct one.* If God is speaking to man in his own language, directing it to his own powers of thinking, and involving his own normal experiences on earth, does it not seem reasonable that we should thus look for the most natural interpretation of a text — unless otherwise indicated? If you come to a passage that has more than one interpretation,

isn't the simplest one most apt to be what the Lord intended?

For example, there are several passages in the New Testament referring to "water" as it relates to a Christian's conversion and life. There are some who insist that it doesn't mean what it says, but really means "word." One passage used is John 3:1-13. They insist that the passage must mean other than what it says. Why? What is wrong with always preferring the more obvious meaning of a passage, unless the context forbids it? Is this not reasonable in any writing or conversing?

3. *Always allow an author's own explanation of a passage to stand*, as over against any other explanation. It is a self-evident fact that a person has a right to explain the way in which he is using an expression. He surely knows what he means better than anyone else does.

Take the word "perfect." Ordinarily, to us the word means "sinless" or "without error." However, the word can also mean "grown up," or "mature in mental or moral judgment." Now in older Bible versions, when we turn to Hebrews 6:1, we know that the writer is urging the Christian to grow unto "perfection" in this latter sense. Why? Read the closing verses of the fifth chapter and note that he explains fully how he uses the word. The NIV properly translates it "maturity."

4. *Always interpret a passage in harmony with the context.* By context we mean the entire section of written thought in which the passage is found. It includes that which immediately precedes and follows and all parts properly connected to it. It may be a paragraph, a chapter, a large section, or the entire writing.

Oh, how much damage has been done to God's truth by snatching passages out of the Bible and using them in ways never intended. This reminds us of the time-worn, humorous example of the man who put together three passages to prove his point: "And Judas "went and hanged himself" (Matthew 27:5); "Go, and do likewise" (Luke 10:37); "What you are about to do, do quickly" (John 13:27). Of course, this is a ridiculous illustration; however, the practice of picking verses at random is all too common.

No, the writings of Scripture demonstrate a continuous, logical flow of thoughts, and a passage should never be forcibly pulled out of this order and forced into the mold of some other thoughts.

Let us consider an example. In John 9:3, Jesus said of the blind man whom He healed, "Neither this man nor his parents sinned." Now, this does not mean that he and his parents were sinless. It simply answers the question as to the cause of his blindness. Read the context, and find that this was said to show that his infirmity was not caused by their sins.

A careful student should seek to determine the general theme of the context, where it begins, where it ends, the general course of thought, and the purpose of the writer.

5. *An interpretation of a passage should always conform to the environment of the author.* What do we mean by this? When an inspired writer recorded the words of the Bible, even though the Holy Spirit gave him the message, he used the conditions of life as he knew them to frame the revealed message. He drew upon the customs of his day, the opinions of his time, the circumstances surrounding his life, and the nature of his own personality. That's why the books of the Bible have different styles of writing and use various expressions and examples, all the while revealing what the Lord intended.

To fully understand any passage of Scripture, the culture of that time and place of writing should be carefully considered, with this important warning: Culture should be taken into account to *illuminate* Scripture, never to *eliminate* Scripture.

6. *Each passage should be interpreted in harmony with all other passages.* This is the normal law of consistency in truth — truth must harmonize with truth. God's Word is truth, and any one portion of it must coincide with everything else He says. God never contradicts Himself.

No two writers have exactly the same minds, nor do they

express truth exactly alike. Therefore, when there seems to be a contradiction between the meanings of passages, one or more of the interpretations must be incorrect. The desire then must be to seek harmony and consistency.

Quite often Romans 3:28 ("A man is justified by faith apart from observing the law") and James 2:24 ("You see that a person is justified by what he does and not by faith alone") are presented as being in conflict. Are they? Read the entire context of both and you will see that they are really complementary, not contradictory. In the light of the authors' purposes, they support one another.

7. Not only is there harmony between passages, but *one passage will often explain another passage.* Paul says that the wisdom that the Holy Spirit teaches compares "spiritual truths in spiritual words" (1 Corinthians 2:13). Do not be too disturbed over a difficult verse (or verses), but plod along in your study. Many times another passage will shed light on the obscure passage and bring forth a sudden flood of understanding. We know more than one instance in which this has happened. An earnest student reports having had trouble with a certain expression, only to have it cleared up only be reading farther on and patiently allowing Scripture to explain Scripture.

However, one word of caution is in order at this point. Such a practice can be overdone by forcing comparisons that are not relative. For instance, some have tried to show the connection and similarity between circumcision and infant baptism, when in fact they differ completely in purpose, in covenant relationship, in action and in Scriptural authority. Likewise, some take the various numbers mentioned in the Bible and force all kinds of comparisons leading to unwarranted conclusions, far beyond what is intended.

8. *A passage must be interpreted in harmony with any idioms it contains* — these are the characteristics peculiar to the original languages of the Bible. One thousand years from now (the Lord willing) what will people think of our common expres-

sion, "OK"? It will be entirely meaningless and mystifying if it has gone out of use by then, unless the interpreters of that time are able to deduce its meaning from today's literature.

The Bible, written in the common languages of man (Hebrew, Aramaic, and Greek), is filled with expressive idioms, and thus our understanding of the meaning of a passage depends upon our understanding the idioms used in it. Modern translations have helped some with this, by translating the meaning of a phrase, rather than exactly word-for-word.

For example, a type of repetition was frequently used in the Hebrew language to give emphasis, as in Genesis 22:17 — "I will surely bless you" — which literally says in the Hebrew (and this is reflected in some older versions), "In blessing I will bless you." Another kind of idiom is found in the "love and hate" expressions. When we read "I loved Jacob, and I hated Esau" (Malachi 1:2,3), it does not mean the contrast of opposites, as the words literally indicate, but it merely denotes a comparison of one being loved more than the other.

9. For a full understanding of the Bible, *all passages on any subject must be studied.* Truth has many sides. Each passage, though true, does not always give all the truth. And usually a passage has a particular design of presenting clearly one facet of truth or of combating some significant extreme people are susceptible to. No one should ever draw a general conclusion on any Bible subject until all passages concerning it have been collected, considered, and compared.

We can think of no better illustration of this than the subject of conversion. In pointing out the steps of salvation that a sinner must take, such passages on faith as John 3:16 and Acts 16:31 have been emphasized by some. On the other hand, such verses on repentance as Luke 13:3, Acts 2:38, and Acts 17:30; on confession of faith as Matthew 10:32 and Romans 10:9,10; and on baptism as Mark 16:16, Acts 2:38, and Acts 22:16 have been put aside. Only the sum total of passages on a given subject will give complete understanding.

10. *Observe the proper balance of Scriptural truth.* Many false doctrines have arisen because some passages have been exaggerated or overemphasized, while others have been slighted. Let the honest student be most careful, weighing out his conclusions so he will be sure to balance the truth as God wills it.

Sometimes the passage itself contains signs of emphasis or urgency, this being done by repetition, sentence structure, and the words themselves. This is not always evident in an English translation, and so the average student may have to use a reliable commentary or several English translations for help in understanding these fine shades of meaning.

11. *Let plain passages determine difficult passages.* All that we need to say here is this: there are some difficult passages that are obscure or hard to understand. They may seem to have more than one meaning. Which is the correct one? Always choose the one that harmonizes with the more plain or easy passages on the same subject. Let definite passages help you understand those that are obscure. Do you find it difficult to grasp what Jesus meant by the expression "born again" (John 3:3-6)? Then get out your concordance and examine each passage in the New Testament on the subject of "birth," "begotten," "conversion," and "salvation."

12. *Correctly understand the book, the dispensations, the covenants, and the settings.* (See chapters 7, 8, 9, and 10.)

13. *Correctly understand the language.* (See chapter 11.)

14. *Know the meaning of words and sentences.* (See chapter 12.)

15. *Know the limits of divine revelation.* (See chapter 13.)

Questions for Review

1. Why are rules necessary?
2. What really are "rules of interpretation"?
3. What is the purpose of rules?
4. What is meant by a passage having only "one meaning"?
5. What do we mean by "the context" where a passage is found?
6. Why seek to harmonize all passages?
7. What is meant by "idioms"?
8. Why is it important to consider all passages on any given subject?

Assignment for Study

Ask eleven students to each explain the meaning of one of the first eleven rules mentioned, showing how it should be applied to any present-day conversation — and then how it should be applied to Scripture.

Topic for Discussion

Indicate some of the unfortunate results that may come from failure to apply any of these rules to Bible study.

CHAPTER SEVEN

The Divisions of the Bible

*"So then, the word of the LORD to them will become: Do and do, do and do,
rule on rule, rule on rule, a little here, a little there"*
(Isaiah 28:13).

This book contains the mind of God, the state of man, the
way of salvation, the doom of sinners, and the happiness of
believers. Its doctrines are holy, its precepts are binding, its
histories are true, and its decisions are immutable. Read it to
be wise, believe in it to be safe, and practice it to be holy. It
contains light to direct you, food to support you, and comfort to cheer you. It is the traveler's map, the pilgrim's staff,
the pilot's compass, the soldier's sword, and the Christian's
charter. Here paradise is restored, heaven opened, and the
gates of hell disclosed. Christ is its grand object, our good its
design, and the glory of God its end. It should fill the memory, rule the heart, and guide the feet. Read it slowly, frequently, and prayerfully. It is a mine of wealth, a paradise of
glory, and a river of pleasure. It is given you in life, will be
opened in the judgment, and be remembered forever. It
involves the highest responsibility, will reward the greatest
labor, and will condemn all who trifle with its sacred contents.   *—Author Unknown*

The Whole Bible

It is amazing how so many authors from several countries,
over a period of so many years, could write so many separate

works and have them end up to be but *one book*. These writers were from many walks of life. They used sermons, poetry, history, prophecy, laws, parables, proverbs, and letters to express their inspired thoughts.

These sixty-six books are separate, yet they are not disconnected fragments. Truth is one harmonious whole, and these separate works all blend into one grand work. It is like a symphony orchestra, each instrument playing its part and making a definite and essential contribution to the overall musical production. Thus the listener is thrilled by the grand presentation of the concert.

In much the same manner, the Bible student must begin by grasping the general view of the entire Bible. It is important to get the right perspective of all the separate parts as they are blended together into one whole. One must see: (1) *The harmony of purpose:* God revealing His will to sinful man in order that he may be saved or redeemed (Ephesians 1:1-23). This purpose, eternal and changeless, runs through the entire course of Scripture. (2) *The harmony of theme:* the history, the nature, and the hope of this grand theme of redemption is the very thing that unites all of these separate books into one Bible. This is not just a collection of moral ideas, good stories, or religious desires. This theme shapes the design of each book, no matter what style or method its author employed. (3) *The harmony of story:* the coming of Jesus Christ is the real story of the whole Bible. It is actually "His-story" (John 20:30,31). How many events, prophecies, characters, and institutions portray some truth in regard to the person or mission of Christ? How much of Christ is entwined throughout the entire Bible record? (4) *The harmony of structure:* every book is essential to the Bible as a whole. Each has its place and function in the total Bible. The separate books are so enmeshed in the whole that to damage or remove any one would injure the unity. The very acceptance of the Bible as it is shows its nature of being a unit. (5) *The harmony of doctrine:* there is one harmonious flow of teaching throughout the Bible. Each law, covenant, commandment, warning, blessing, etc., has its designed place, producing a unity that attests to the divine authorship from beginning to end.

Fix firmly in your mind, in concise but flowing terms and thoughts, the general story of the entire Bible. Here is such an attempt:

In the beginning God created the heavens and the earth, and all the living creatures including man. Man sinned and spoiled the kind of life God intended him to live. Therefore, God designed and began the long unfolding of His plan to redeem man from the curse of his sin. Through the family first, then through a chosen nation, God progressively revealed His will. This nation, Israel, through whom the Redeemer, or Savior, was repeatedly promised, grew into a great power, later divided, fell into captivity, and finally was partially restored to the Promised Land. Some four hundred years after the Old Testament closed, the time was fulfilled and the Savior came into the world. He lived, taught, suffered, died on the cross, arose from the dead, and returned to the Father. Then the Holy Spirit was sent to guide those selected to preach the good news of salvation, direct the establishment of the community (the church) of the saved, and instruct in the nature of godly living. The New Testament record ends with the work of human redemption well under way throughout the world at that time, and a brief view is given of the Christian hope.

In Genesis we see the creation of the heavens and the earth; in Revelation, the creation of the new heaven and the new earth.

In Genesis we see the beginning of sin; in Revelation, the destruction of sin.

In Genesis we see the beginning of pain, sorrow and death; in Revelation, the end of pain, sorrow, and death.

In Genesis we see man deprived of the tree of life and driven out of the garden; in Revelation, man is invited to eat of the tree of life and live forever in the garden.

In Genesis we see Satan enter, deceive man, and the world; in Revelation, Satan is overthrown and cast out forever.

In Genesis we see man go from life to death; in Revelation, we see man go from death to life.

In Genesis man first says to the Lord, "I was afraid"; in Revelation, his last words are: "Amen. Come, Lord Jesus."

The Two Testaments

We have begun with the Bible in its entirety. Now let us begin to divide it correctly. A logical breaking down of the various parts and division of the Bible is vital. This will be done progressively until we have reached the several divisions in particular.

Of course, we begin with the two main divisions: the Old Testament and the New Testament. Basically, the thirty-nine books of the Old Testament were written to guide people before the coming of Christ, while the twenty-seven books of the New Testament are directed to all people living since the Savior came. The word "testament" means "will." There is a significance in the words "old" and "new."

The Eight Divisions

The next step is to classify each of the two Testaments into their four respective divisions. Remember, the books of the Bible are not arranged strictly in the order in which they were written, but according to the nature of their contents. They appear in a logical order first, then somewhat chronological.

Now, carefully study the chart opposite. Commit to memory the four divisions of the Old Testament, along with the number of books in each. Also, do the same for the New Testament. Then be able to show how the Bible naturally divides itself so as to point to the Lord Jesus Christ, who is the center of all God's revelation.

DIVISIONS OF THE BIBLE

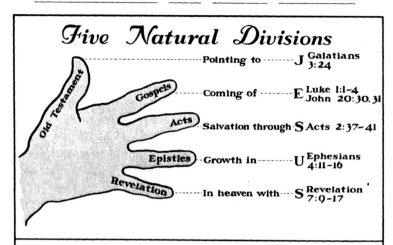

Five Natural Divisions

Old Testament	Pointing to	J Galatians 3:24
Gospels	Coming of	E Luke 1:1-4 / John 20:30, 31
Acts	Salvation through	S Acts 2:37-41
Epistles	Growth in	U Ephesians 4:11-16
Revelation	In heaven with	S Revelation 7:9-17

Old Testament

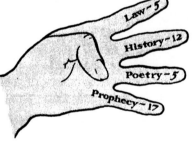

Law - 5
History - 12
Poetry - 5
Prophecy - 17

New Testament

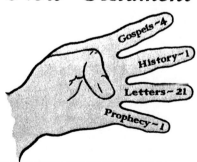

Gospels - 4
History - 1
Letters - 21
Prophecy - 1

BOOKS OF THE BIBLE

Old Testament
39 Books

LAW — 5
- Genesis
- Exodus
- Leviticus
- Numbers
- Deuteronomy

HISTORY — 12
- Joshua
- Judges
- Ruth
- 1 Samuel
- 2 Samuel
- 1 Kings
- 2 Kings
- 1 Chronicles
- 2 Chronicles
- Ezra
- Nehemiah
- Esther

POETRY — 5
- Job
- Psalms
- Proverbs
- Ecclesiastes
- Song of Solomon

MAJOR PROPHETS — 5
- Isaiah
- Jeremiah
- Lamentations
- Ezekiel
- Daniel

MINOR PROPHETS — 12
- Hosea
- Joel
- Amos
- Obadiah
- Jonah
- Micah
- Nahum
- Habakkuk
- Zephaniah
- Haggai
- Zechariah
- Malachi

New Testament
27 Books

GOSPELS — 4
- Matthew
- Mark
- Luke
- John

HISTORY — 1
- Acts

LETTERS — 21
- Romans
- 1 Corinthians
- 2 Corinthians
- Galatians
- Ephesians
- Philippians
- Colossians
- 1 Thessalonians
- 2 Thessalonians
- 1 Timothy
- 2 Timothy
- Titus
- Philemon
- Hebrews
- James
- 1 Peter
- 2 Peter
- 1 John
- 2 John
- 3 John
- Jude

PROPHECY — 1
- Revelation

The Sixty-six Books

Finally, we must now catalog the entire library of sixty-six books. It would be well to memorize them, a job not too difficult, and, oh, so rewarding. Look at the chart. The writer has found this to be the best way to learn the books of the Bible. Notice how the books are listed in each division. It is orderly, systematic, and conducive to good memory work; it produces a photographic image for the mind to use and retain.

Let us now list all the Bible books and attempt to give the gist of each in one sentence or less:

Genesis: The beginning of the world, man, the family, sin, and the chosen nation; from the creation through the life of Joseph.

Exodus: The chosen people are led out of Egypt by Moses and given the law (including the Ten Commandments) and the tabernacle.

Leviticus: The ceremonial law, in regard to sacrifices, the priesthood, and holy seasons.

Numbers: The forty-year wanderings of Israel in the wilderness and a census of the people.

Deuteronomy: A rehearsal of Israel's history, laws and warnings.

Joshua: The conquest of Canaan with the tribes settling in the land.

Judges: The rule of the judges, with oppressions and deliverances, from Joshua to Samson.

Ruth: The ancestry of the Messianic family.

1 Samuel: The founding of the Hebrew kingdom under Saul and David.

2 Samuel: The reign of David.

1 Kings: The "golden age" of the kingdom under Solomon, with the beginning of division and decay.

2 Kings: The divided kingdom to the captivities of both the northern and southern tribes.

1 Chronicles: Hebrew history, including the reign of David.

2 Chronicles: Further Hebrew history under Solomon, and the history of Judah after the division.

Ezra: The return from captivity in Babylon and the rebuilding of the temple.

Nehemiah: The rebuilding of the walls of Jerusalem.

Esther: The Jews are delivered from destruction by a Hebrew maiden who became queen of Persia.

Job: The problem of human suffering through the trials and triumph of Job.

Psalms: A collection of poems and hymns used by the Hebrews for praise and worship.

Proverbs: A collection of wise sayings about the practical issues of life.

Ecclesiastes: A poem dealing with the search for happiness.

Song of Solomon: A poem of love and longing.

Isaiah: Exhortations on repentance and predictions on the coming Messiah.

Jeremiah: Warnings to Jerusalem about the Babylonian captivity and approaching suffering.

Lamentations: Poems lamenting the destruction of Jerusalem.

Ezekiel: Visions of judgment and the restoration of Israel.

Daniel: The story of the captives in Babylon, including Daniel.

Hosea: Denouncement of Israel and prediction of Jerusalem's destruction.

Joel: Predictions concerning the coming day of God.

Amos: Prophecies denouncing apostasy and wickedness, predicting punishment and final restoration of Israel.

Obadiah: The doom of Edom.

Jonah: Prophecies concerning Nineveh; the prophet's errand and error.

Micah: Prophecy concerning the fall of Israel and Judah.

Nahum: Doom of Nineveh.

Habakkuk: The invasion of Judah and destruction of Chaldeans foretold.

Zephaniah: Destruction and restoration of Judah foretold.

Haggai: Urgency of rebuilding the temple.

Zechariah: Rebuilding the temple and predictions of coming Messiah.

Malachi: Denunciation of vice and warnings to repent.

Matthew: The life of Jesus, the Messiah.

Mark: The life of Jesus, the worker of wonders.

Luke: The life of Jesus, the Son of man.

John: The life of Jesus, the Son of God.

Acts: The beginning and spread of the gospel and of the church under the apostles.

Romans: Fundamental issues of the Christian faith.

1 Corinthians: Correction of several church disorders.

2 Corinthians: A vindication of Paul's apostleship and further reproof and instruction.

Galatians: Salvation is by grace, not by law.

Ephesians: The glory of redemption and the real unity of the church.

Philippians: Christian testimony of love, gratitude, and encouragement to the faithful.

Colossians: The supremacy of Christ.

1 Thessalonians: The Lord's return.

2 Thessalonians: Further instruction on the return of Christ.

1 and 2 Timothy: Instructions to a young evangelist.

Titus: Instructions to a young evangelist.

Philemon: Letter concerning a runaway slave.

Hebrews: The superiority of the New Covenant over the Old.

James: Christian wisdom and good works.

1 Peter: Encouragement to persecuted Christians.

2 Peter: Prediction of apostasy.

1 John: Christian love and conduct.

2 and 3 John: Caution against false teachers, and confidence in the faithful.

Jude: Warning against false teachers.

Revelation: Ultimate overthrow of Satan and final triumph of Christ and His faithful.

One last division should be noted, that of chapters and verses. It must be remembered, however, that this was not in the original. This is man's addition to the Bible, first appearing in the whole Bible in the sixteenth century. Therefore, it is a useful tool as one searches the Word, but should never interfere with the work of interpreting. This is a human division, and sometimes not very accurate. For example, breaking the thought in Ephesians 1:15-2:7 or 1 Corinthians 12, 13 and 14 by chapter divisions, has often impaired the understanding of these passages. Use the divisions, but do not be a slave to them.

Questions for Review

1. Why is it important to grasp the general meaning of the whole Bible?
2. What is the grand theme and purpose of the Bible?
3. Basically, what is the difference between the two Testaments?
4. In what order are the separate books placed in the Bible?
5. What are the five ways in which the Bible is harmonized?
6. What advantage and disadvantage is there to the chapter and verse divisions in the Bible?

Assignment for Study

Be able to give from memory all eight divisions of the Bible, along with the list of books in each.

Topic for Discussion

See who in class can best tell the whole Bible story in less than two hundred words — complete but concise.

CHAPTER EIGHT

The Periods of Revelation

*"In reading this, then, you will be able to understand my insight into
the mystery of Christ, which was not made known to men
in other generations as it has now been revealed . . ."
(Ephesians 3:4,5).*

We have taken the Bible apart section by section and book by book. Now let us put it back together, not in the order of *books*, but according to *time*. The Bible is God's story, and a story is the weaving together of persons and events in an orderly and meaningful pattern. There is a message and a purpose in it. All that we have said is true of the Scriptures. Now then, let us take the various books, or parts of books, and weave them together into the long narrative that covers thousands of years. Let us allow God to tell His whole story in the order in which it actually happened.

Three Basic Periods

In reading God's story as recorded in the various kinds of writings (law, history, prophecy, biography, epistle, etc.), we find that it falls into three general periods of time or ages. These are often called "dispensations." A dispensation means a period of time during which God reveals a certain area of His will, and deals with man in a particular way. Each of these should be identified, with their essential characteristics noted.

1. *Patriarchal Age.* This name comes from word roots meaning "father" and "rule." In the early dawn of history, God began to deal with man as the head of his family. Instead of revealing a written code of law and system of worship, He spoke to the fathers through visions, dreams, and angels. We know little about this period, even though we see, gradually unfolded, some fundamental truth on life and worship. For example, the doctrine of sacrifice begins to appear. Because of the limitation and nature of God's revelation through this long age, lasting thousands of years, it has been called the "Starlight Age."

2. *Mosaic Age.* Here the name springs from the great lawgiver, Moses. During this period God expanded His method of dealing with man by choosing a nation (Israel). Man was now ready for more revelation; hence this is called the "Moonlight Age." Through Moses, God set down a definite written code for social, political, and religious life, with the Ten Commandments as its center. Now appeared the doctrines of the priesthood, sacrifice, holy days and seasons, and sacrifices in the tabernacle. Also, a nation was taught law and order, with her record of obedience and disobedience, along with corresponding rewards and punishments. This period lasted about fifteen hundred years.

3. *Christian Age.* The name here, of course, refers to Christ, the "author and finisher" in the story of God's revelation. The chief characteristic here is that God turns from a family and a nation to the whole world. Now the grand purpose of God is fulfilled through His Son: the redemption of all mankind on earth (those who are willing to be saved). This is done through the "perfect law of liberty." Thus, it is the "Sunlight Age" — the present age in which we live. More than nineteen hundred years have transpired thus far.

Outline and Chart

In making a further breakdown of these three basic periods of time, we shall use two effective tools — an outline and a chart. If these are clearly fixed in one's mind and properly interpreted, their value will be immeasurable to the Bible student.

First, study the following outline carefully. Notice the unfolding, period by period, of the story of God. Each includes the dates (some have to be approximate), the number of years covered, and the books of the Bible that reveal that portion of the study.

Next, review the chart. Imagine this as being one long chart to portray the span of all centuries. For the sake of space, this is broken up into six units and placed on two pages. Through these we have tried to show where the books of the Bible come into the story. The vertical lines indicate the dates in history, B.C. on the first four units, and A.D. on the last two. According to our calendar, due to an error made years ago, Christ probably was born in 4 B.C. The breakdown of the various periods is indicated underneath each unit. Then, note the name of each book of the Bible and the line underneath it. In the case of a law, a historical or a biographical writing, the line represents that period of time that its narrative covers. In regard to prophecies, devotional books, and epistles, their lines simply indicate the approximate times when these books were written.

Even though we cannot be exact in regard to some of the dates, nevertheless, such a cataloging proves the most helpful to our understanding of the Bible. Fasten as much of these two helps in your mind as possible. Then, have them accessible in much of your Bible study. It will help make the individual books and passages come alive with meaning. To see the writings in their relative settings and as parts of the whole story will enrich your Bible understanding.

BIBLE OUTLINE

PATRIARCHAL AGE (Genesis 1–Exodus 19)
  Preflood Period (No definite dates can be established)
    Genesis 1:1–8:12
  Postflood Period (No definite dates can be established)
    Genesis 8:13–11:26
  Abrahamic Period (c. 2100-1877 B.C., 223 years)
    Genesis 11:27–50:26; Job?
  Period of Bondage (c. 1877-1447 B.C., 430 years)
    Exodus 1–19
MOSAIC AGE (Exodus 20–Acts 1)
  Period of Wanderings (1447–1407 B.C., 40 years)
    Exodus 20–40; Leviticus; Numbers; Deuteronomy
  Period of Conquest (1407–1367 B.C., 40 years)
    Joshua
  Period of Judges (1367–1050 B.C., 317 years)
    Judges; Ruth; 1 Samuel 1–10
  Period of the United Kingdom (1050–931 B.C., 120 years)
    1 Samuel 11–31; 2 Samuel; 1 Kings 1–11; 1 Chronicles;
    2 Chronicles 1–10; Psalms (some uncertain); Proverbs;
    Ecclesiastes; Song of Solomon
  Period of the Divided Kingdom (931–587 B.C., 344 years)
    1. Period of Northern Kingdom (931–722 B.C., 209 years)
      1 Kings 12–22; 2 Kings 1–17; Hosea; Amos; Jonah
    2. Period of Southern Kingdom (931–587 B.C., 344 years)
      1 Kings 12–22; 2 Kings 1–24; 2 Chronicles 10–36;
      Isaiah; Jeremiah; Joel; Obadiah; Micah; Nahum;
      Habakkuk; Zephaniah
  Period of Exile (587–536 B.C., 50 years)
    2 Kings 25; 2 Chronicles 36; Lamentations; Ezekiel;
    Daniel
  Post-Exile Period (536–431 B.C., 136 years)
    Ezra; Nehemiah; Esther; Haggai; Zechariah; Malachi
  Between the Testaments (431–4 B.C., 427 years)
    No Bible record

Period of Christ's Life and Work (4 B.C.–A.D. 30, 33 ½ years)
    Matthew; Mark; Luke; John; Acts 1
      1. Preparation, thirty years
      2. Obscurity, one year
      3. Popularity, one year
      4. Opposition, one year
      5. Persecution, three months
      6. Sacrifice, one week
      7. Victory, forty days

CHRISTIAN AGE (Acts 2–Revelation 22)
  Period of Apostles' Work (A.D. 30–100, 70 years)
      1. Founding & Growth of the Church (A.D. 30–100, 70 yrs)
         Acts 2–7
      2. Extension of the Church to Judea, Samaria, and to the
         Gentiles (A.D. 35–45)
         Acts 8–12
      3. Paul's Missionary Tours Among the Gentiles (A.D. 45–58)
         Acts 13:1–21:26; Romans; 1 & 2 Corinthians; 1 & 2
         Thessalonians; Galatians; James
      4. Paul's Imprisonment (A.D. 58–63)
         Acts 21:27–28:31; Ephesians; Philippians; Colossians;
         Philemon; Hebrews
      5. Later Apostolic History (A.D. 63–100)
         1 & 2 Timothy; Titus; 1 & 2 Peter; 1, 2, & 3 John; Jude;
         Revelation

OLD TESTAMENT HISTORY
Before Christ
(No definite dates can be established)

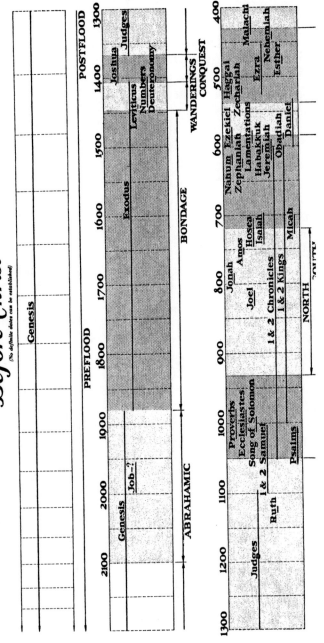

BETWEEN THE TESTAMENTS
Before Christ

NEW TESTAMENT HISTORY
After Christ

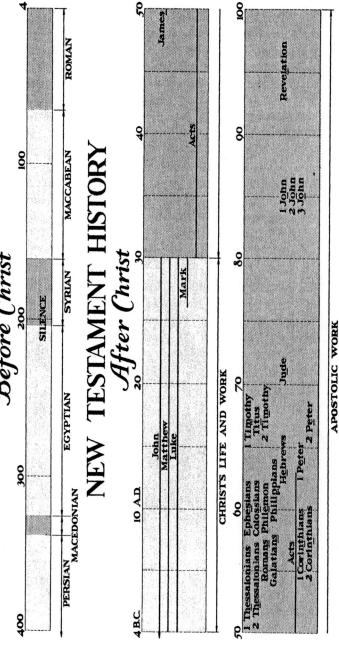

Questions for Review

1. What does the word "dispensation" mean?
2. How many basic periods of Bible history are there?
3. Name them and tell what each means.
4. What are the essential characteristics of each?
5. Tell how long each period lasted.
6. What is meant by the "Starlight," "Moonlight," and "Sunlight" ages?

Assignment for Study

Memorize the outline of Bible history, at least committing to memory the names of the main divisions of time and the fifteen subdivisions. Be able to recite them to yourself or in class.

Topic for Discussion

The following will help a student relate Bible truth to the truth as a whole, and grasp its vastness of theme and sequence of thought and purpose. Pick out a number of important Bible persons, things, and events. Then as you call them out to students, in turn, see if they can relate them to their proper age and period.

CHAPTER NINE

The Covenants Within the Bible

"But the ministry Jesus has received is as superior to theirs as the covenant of which he is mediator is superior to the old one, and it is founded on better promises. For if there had been nothing wrong with that first covenant, no place would have been sought for another"
(Hebrews 8:6,7).

We have taken the Bible apart *book* by *book*, and have studied the contents by *periods* of time. Now let us see this story unfold in another way, according to the personal relationship between God the author and man the reader. We must see the gradual development or stages of this relationship if we wish to understand the grand purpose and message of the Bible.

God Progressively Deals With Man

Man was created, and right away he alienated himself from the Creator by sinning. What was God to do? He could not begin to tell man everything at once, no more than a parent can teach his child everything at once. There must be a gradual unfolding, explaining, repeating, and correcting, measured out according to the maturing of the one taught. The teacher must hand out just that portion of truth that is needed and is digestible.

The Bible is such a record of how God has gradually

revealed His will to man. It is composed of many parts of the whole truth, even though one part may be more primitive or undeveloped than another. Truth was to come like the flower — first the blade, then the stem, then the bud, and then the full bloom. We must remember this when we examine any given passage. Where in the unfolding of God's dealing with man does it occur? Remember, one stroke of a brush does not make a painting, one note does not make a symphony nor does one page make a book. This does not mean that God tries one thing, and then when that fails pursues another. Neither does it indicate that the book grows from error to truth. It simply means that God imparts His will to man as fast as man can accept it. A century may intervene between the revelation of two parts of a truth, but God waits until man is ready.

As our nation prepared to lift a man into orbit around the earth, it took time. Thousands of people expended talent and energy to prepare for the countdown. Millions of dollars were spent. Every instrument and condition had to be just right. The author lives in a community where one small but important piece of equipment was designed and proudly engineered to fit into the space helmet of the first U.S. astronaut to circle the globe. Whether small or big, each part is essential. So it is with God's eternal purpose toward man. Out of love for His creation He proceeds step by step to deal with man. Each arrangement or compact is called a "covenant."

These Covenants Must Be Outlined

A covenant is a solemn agreement or compact entered into by two parties, binding them together to do things on behalf of each other. A marriage license, a union work contract, a deed to a piece of land, a loan from the bank, and even a public library card are cases of covenants in everyday life. In the Bible use of the term, when referring to the God-man relationship, it means that God takes the leadership as the superior, and graciously enters into a relationship with man, whereby promises are fulfilled when certain holy conditions are met. Sometimes the word "testament" is used. Actually, both words are used interchangeably. However, a testament or will is a specific kind of covenant whereby one must die before the promises are realized. The gospel is rightly called the New Testament in that Christ had to die before it could come into force (Hebrews 9:16,17). In like manner, that particular covenant referred to as the Law of Moses may be called an Old Testament, for it took the blood of beasts (Hebrews 9:19,20) to ratify it.

A covenant has four essential parts. There is (1) the first party — the covenanter, or benefactor; (2) the second party — the covenantee, or beneficiary; (3) the conditions that have to be met, conditions that are fair, wise, holy, and of course, possible; and finally (4) promises or blessings to be desired and received, after the conditions are met. A young man offers his love, filled with many promises; but unless the young lady responds in like manner, assenting to a marriage covenant, there will be no marriage, with all of its blessings.

Now the Bible is the record of such a series of contracts or covenants that God made, each being offered at a certain time and to certain persons, in order to accomplish certain purposes. The Bible is not primarily a book of history, science, or religious thoughts, but a record of divine covenants. We are now ready to outline six important covenants. These are not the only ones recorded. There are others, some between two persons. However, these are the fundamental arrangements that carry on God's progressive dealings with man, and which thus affect our understanding the Bible.

Note the different parts of each covenant. Some have a mediator between the two parties involved. There is a token of each, serving as a mark or sign of evidence. Then too, it is well to note that actually there is one general condition that runs through all covenants God made with man: man must believe in God and love and obey Him (Matthew 22:36-40;

Hebrews 11:6). Watch how God has dictated different ways for this to be expressed in the various covenants.

COVENANT WITH ADAM

1. *First Party – Benefactor*
   God (Genesis 1:28,29; 2:15,16).
2. *Second Party – Beneficiaries*
   Adam and Eve (Genesis 1:26,27; 2:16).
3. *Conditions*
   "Be fruitful, and increase in number" (Genesis 1:28).
   "Fill the earth" (Genesis 1:28).
   "Subdue it: and rule over . . . every living creature" (Genesis 1:28).
   Dress and keep the garden (Genesis 2:15).
   Do not eat "from the tree of the knowledge of good and evil" (Genesis 2:17).
4. *Promises*
   Given the garden to live in, and every herb and tree for food (Genesis 1:29; 2:8,9,16).
   "The tree of life" (Genesis 2:9,16).
5. *Mediator*
   None
6. *Token*
   Man created in God's image (Genesis 1:26,27).

COVENANT WITH NOAH
Before the Flood

1. *First Party – Benefactor*
   God (Genesis 6:13).
2. *Second Party – Beneficiaries*
   Noah, his wife, their three sons and their wives (Genesis 6:13,18; 7:13).
3. *Conditions*
   Build an ark (Genesis 6:14-16).

Enter in with family (Genesis 6:18; 7:1).

Gather certain number of beasts, fowls, and creeping things (Genesis 6:19,20; 7:2,3).

Gather food to eat (Genesis 6:21).

4. *Promises*

Noah's family saved from death (Genesis 7:23).

5. *Mediator*

None

6. *Token*

The flood (Genesis 7:10-12, 17-24).

COVENANT WITH NOAH
After the Flood

1. *First Party – Benefactor*

God (Genesis 9:8,12).

2. *Second Party – Beneficiaries*

Noah and his seed after him (Genesis 9:8-10).

3. *Conditions*

"Be fruitful and increase in number and fill the earth" (Genesis 9:1,7).

"But you must not eat meat that has its lifeblood still in it" (Genesis 9:4).

"Whoever sheds the blood of man, by man shall his blood be shed" (Genesis 9:6).

4. *Promises*

God will not "curse the ground" any more (Genesis 8:21).

Nor "destroy all living creatures" (Genesis 8:21).

Days and seasons will not cease (Genesis 8:22).

Man shall rule beasts, fowls and fishes (Genesis 9:2).

Both animals and plants for food (Genesis 9:3).

No more flood to destroy the earth (Genesis 9:11).

5. *Mediator*

None

6. *Token*

God set the rainbow in the clouds (Genesis 9:12-17).

COVENANT WITH ABRAHAM

1. *First Party – Benefactor*
   God (Genesis 12:1; 17:1-3).
2. *Second Party – Beneficiaries*
   Abraham and his descendants to follow in all generations (Genesis 17:7).
3. *Conditions*
   Go out of the country into a new land God would show (Genesis 12:1).

   Walk before God and be blameless (Genesis 17:1).

   Offer his son, Isaac, for a burnt offering (Genesis 22:2).
4. *Promises*
   God would make of him a great nation (Genesis 12:2).

   God would bless him and make his name great (Genesis 12:2).

   "I will bless those who bless you, and whoever curses you I will curse" (Genesis 12:3).

   In him all the families of the earth would be blessed (Genesis 12:3; 22:18).

   "Unto your offspring I will give this land" (Genesis 12:7).

   God would make his offspring as the dust of the earth (Genesis 13:16).

   Abraham would have a son (Genesis 15:4).

   He would be the father of many nations (Genesis 17:4).

   God would be a God to him, and his descendants (Genesis 17:7).

   His descendants would possess the cities of his enemies (Genesis 22:17).

   God would give them Egypt to sojourn in (Genesis 26:1-5).

   God would return Abraham's descendants to the Promised Land (Genesis 28:10-15).
5. *Mediator*
   None

6. *Token*

Circumcision (Genesis 17:10-14).

THE LAW

1. *First Party – Benefactor*

God (Exodus 20:1).

2. *Second Party – Beneficiaries*

All Israel (Exodus 34:27; Deuteronomy 5:1-3).

3. *Conditions*

The Ten Commandments, plus all the statutes and judgments pertaining to private, social (or political), and religious life (Exodus 20 through Deuteronomy).

4. *Promises*

Israel shall be a kingdom of priests and a holy nation (Exodus 19:5.6).

God will give (Deuteronomy 26):

Good harvests and ample food

Safety and peace

Deliverance from evil beasts

Protection from and power over enemies

Respect

Growth in number

His presence

5. *Mediator*

Moses (Deuteronomy 5:5).

6. *Token*

Sabbath (Exodus 31:12-17; Ezekiel 20:12,20).

THE GOSPEL

1. *First Party – Benefactor*

God (Romans 1:1,16; Hebrews 1:1,2).

2. *Second Party – Beneficiaries*

All the world (Matthew 28:19; Mark 16:15,16).

3. *Conditions*

Hear the gospel (Romans 10:13,14; 1 Corinthians 15:1).

Believe in Jesus Christ (Mark 16:15,16; John 20:30,31; Acts 8:36,37; Romans 10:13,14; 1 Corinthians 1:21; Hebrews 11:6).

Repent of sin (Luke 24:47; Acts 2:38; 17:30).

Confess faith in Jesus Christ (Acts 8:37; Romans 10:10; Philippians 2:11).

Be baptized into Christ (Matthew 28:19; Mark 16:16; Acts 2:38; 8:36-39; 9:18; 22:16; Galatians 3:27).

Continue to grow in holiness as a Christian (Matthew 28:20; 2 Corinthians 7:1; 1 Peter 2:1-3; 2 Peter 1:5-11); by worshiping the Lord (Acts 2:42; Hebrews 10:24-26); by praying and studying His Word (1 Thessalonians 5:17; 1 Timothy 2:8; 2 Timothy 2:15; 1 Peter 2:2; 1 John 1:9); by testifying to all men (Matthew 28:19; Acts 8:1-3, 29, 35; Colossians 3:16); by being a good steward of all life (1 Corinthians 4:1,2; 6:19,20; 16:2; 1 Peter 4:10); and remaining faithful until death (Revelation 2:10).

4. *Promises*

Forgiveness (Ephesians 1:7; Colossians 1:14).

Election (Romans 8:33).

Redemption (Romans 3:23-26).

Justification (Romans 8:1,30,31).

Grace (Ephesians 2:8,9; 2 Timothy 2:1).

Salvation (2 Timothy 2:10).

Hope (1 Thessalonians 1:3; Ephesians 1:12).

Peace (Romans 5:1; 1 Peter 5:14).

Wisdom (James 1:5).

Protection and help (1 Corinthians 10:13; Philippians 4:19).

Righteousness (Romans 3:21,22; 5:17).

Inheritance (Galatians 3:26-29).

Rest (Revelation 14:13).

Victory (2 Corinthians 2:14).

Glory (2 Timothy 2:10).

Eternal life (Romans 6:23; 1 John 5:11).

5. *Mediator*

Jesus Christ (1 Timothy 2:5; Hebrews 9:15).

6. *Token*

Gift of the Holy Spirit (Acts 2:38; 2 Corinthians 1:22; Galatians 5:22-25; Ephesians 1:13; 4:30).

These Covenants Must Be Divided

One of the chief causes of misunderstanding the Bible has been the failure to keep these covenants separate. Zealous readers have taken parts from different covenants and put them together to build or defend a doctrine. The mixing of these can do nothing else but produce confusion. Especially this has been true of the law and the gospel. Here are two separate covenants, the intermingling of which has resulted in all kinds of error.

It is important that we know where to draw the lines separating the covenants. Jesus himself lived under the former covenant. When He died this brought an end to, and the fulfillment of (Matthew 5:17) the law (Colossians 2:14; Hebrews 10:9,10). This could be likened to a labor union contract. No matter how good the one is, a better one written and ratified later on takes the place of the old one.

The Old Testament was as inspired as the New. However, the law was faulty, not because God erred and needed to make another try, but because of man's nature (Hebrews 8:6,7). So this covenant was a long, elaborate means by which God would be able to prepare man for the final, perfect covenant, the gospel (Galatians 2:16,21; 3:24).

The difference between these two major covenants is quite significant. The law was a strict legal code, which a man was supposed to obey in its entirety. However, no man, except Jesus, has ever done so. Under a strictly legalistic system an individual is accepted purely on the basis of his own merit or achievement. This was the method or principle by which God dealt with man under the law. Under the gospel, it is not so much a difference in the standard of right and wrong as it is a new principle of life. Now man simply casts himself on Jesus Christ and His righteousness through faith and obedience. This in turn fills his soul with new power, a different kind of control, enabling him to do more of the law than man has ever been able to do before. In addition, where he, the Christian, fails to meet all the demands of the law, the grace of God reaches down and forgives. This is why it is called the "good news." The law never could do this. It was never intended that it function in this manner (Romans 3:20,23; Hebrews 10:1-4).

Today we are no longer under the law, or any of the former covenants, but solely under the New Testament (Romans 6:14; 7:4-6; Hebrews 7:18,19; 10:9,10). We rejoice in the system of grace (unmerited favor of God). It enables us to meet more of God's demands for holiness, and although we are unable to earn God's favor, we nevertheless receive it by grace. God made several covenants or wills. We are under only one of them — the last and final one — and that is most important.

Questions for Review

1. What is meant by saying that the Bible is a "progressive" revelation?
2. What is the meaning of the word "covenant"? "testament"?
3. Give an example of a covenant in everyday life, other than those mentioned in this chapter.
4. Name the four essential parts of a covenant, and show the importance of each part.
5. Define "mediator" and "token."
6. Name the six major Bible covenants mentioned in this chapter.
7. Why do you think it is important to distinguish between the Bible covenants?

Assignment for Study

On a piece of paper, or on the chalkboard, divide the space in two by drawing a vertical line down the center. Now list as many of the six points of the law (on one side) and the gospel (on the other) as you can and compare them.

Topic for Discussion

Discuss as many ways as you can in which the gospel is superior to the law.

CHAPTER TEN

The Importance of Setting

"In the past God spoke to our forefathers through the prophets at many times and in various ways . . ."
(Hebrews 1:1).

RULES OF INTERPRETATION

It shall greatly help thee to understand Scripture,
If thou mark
Not only what is spoken or written,
But of whom,
And to whom,
With what words,
At what time,
Where,
With what circumstances,
Considering what goeth before
And what followeth.

The poem, written by an unnamed Bible scholar, is about four hundred years old. It would be difficult today to pen a better rule for the student to memorize and put to use. Let us see what it means.

We want to understand the message of the Bible. It is God's Word as delivered by the Holy Spirit. We ask, "What is the Holy Spirit really trying to tell us?" Certainly, in all fairness to Him whom God has appointed to be our guide and teacher in all matters vital to our spiritual welfare, we should be most careful to keep all words in their setting as they were first given. When we come to a certain passage and carefully analyze it, we are, in a sense, lifting it out of the Bible. But to properly know its meaning, we must put it back again. It is not enough, however, just to return it to its place according to chapter and verse. But in the spirit of the last two lessons, we must put it in its rightful place, according to the period of time and the covenant involved. This involves the all-important issue of seeing it in its original, thus true, environment. We must be fully aware of its entire setting wherein the Holy Spirit first placed it. Many times there are passages that are exactly alike in words but quite different in meanings, this being made clear by ascertaining the particular setting of each. This is called making an "historical approach" to Bible study.

For example, as young people many of us learned to sing this little chorus:

> Every promise in the book is mine,
> Every chapter, every verse, every line,
> All are blessings of His love divine,
> Every promise in the Book is mine.

But after a while, we learned that this actually was not quite true. There are many promises in the Bible that were never given to us of today. Some chapters, verses, and lines were not intended for Christians to follow. So we changed the chorus to read:

> Many a promise in the Book is mine,
> Many a chapter, many a verse, many a line.
> All are blessings of His love divine,
> Many a promise in the Book is mine.

Now this is right, and this is true of more than just promises. Every fact, commandment, prohibition, warning, exhortation, example, prophecy, and promise must be carefully placed in its proper setting to be correctly understood. This can be done by asking the following seven questions about any passage in question.

Who Is Speaking or Writing?

In general, it is well to look behind the writing and recognize the writer. Who is he? What is his place in God's plan? In each case it is an inspired man. However, his peculiar position is important.

Being more specific, we now ask in a given passage, "Who is speaking?" Here we find there can be a number of possibilities. Is it an angel or a demon? Is the writer quoting the devil? This was done more than once (Genesis 3:1-5; Matthew 4:3-11). Is it the word of God or man? We read one passage that says that Job was "a blameless and an upright man" (Job 1:8), while another declares his "wickedness" to be "great" (Job 22:5). What is the difference? The first was a quotation from God and the second fell from the lips of a man, Eliphaz.

If the person speaking is a man, is he inspired or not? If inspired, then God really is the author. However, if the one speaking is not inspired, then we should ask, "Who is he?" He could be an ordinary voice on the street, a Pharisee, a false prophet, a Jew or Gentile, a Sadducee, a pagan king, a mistaken "good person," a man or woman, etc. Why, the Bible even contains some lies (Genesis 3:4; Matthew 12:24; John 7:20). Yes, even words from the worst of men will be quoted in Scripture because God wanted them faithfully recorded for our good. But we must be careful to ask, "Who is speaking?"

William W. Orr tells the story of a murder case being tried in the South.

> Without a doubt the defendant was guilty, but the lawyer was clever. Addressing the jury, he pleaded self-defense for his client, quoting the "highest authority" in the world, citing

the Bible where it is said, ". . . all that a man hath will he give for his life." The jury was impressed.

But the prosecuting lawyer knew his Bible, and when it came his turn to speak, he pointed out devastatingly the one whom the opposing attorney considered to be the highest authority in the world by quoting from Job 2:4: "And Satan . . . said, . . . all that a man hath will he give for his life."[1]

To Whom?

It makes quite a difference in the meaning of a passage when one considers to whom it is addressed. This is true of any message. Sometimes a Bible message was directed to only one individual, as in the case of Nathan's message to David (2 Samuel 12:7); to a certain group of people, to a nation of people, or to the whole world. Of course, some of these are determined by other questions asked in this chapter.

There are times when specific classes of persons are addressed. For example, there are some words directed to Christians, but to specified kinds of Christians, such as apostles (Matthew 10:19), elders (Acts 20:17-35), evangelists (2 Timothy 4:2), husbands, wives, children, slaves, and masters (Ephesians ch. 5,6). There was even personal instruction to those who had been granted special powers of the Holy Spirit (1 Corinthians ch. 12,14). Words thus directed to certain parties must include them, and only them, unless otherwise stated.

The writer approached a home once, and was about to ring the doorbell when he saw a note tacked on the door. It contained instructions to "come on in and wait" for the party to return, and the note was signed. However, there was one more thing of importance — it was not for me, because it was addressed to another person. This made the note an entirely different message.

---

[1]William W. Orr, *Bible Study Is Easy* (Wheaton, IL: Scripture Press), p. 27.

About Whom?

After asking who spoke and to whom, it is well then to ask, "About whom was this said?" That is, a third party may be involved. God frequently used this method. For example, when God gave the Ten Commandments to Moses, all of Israel and their descendants were involved. It was not Moses alone who was responsible to the law. A great deal of misunderstanding is created when the wrong third party is claimed as the object of a certain teaching.

Read Mark 16:15-18. Some would have these promises of divine powers or signs pertain to everyone who believes and is baptized. However, such gifts of healing and signs of miracles were not given to all Christians in all times. Other passages (Acts 8:14-19; 1 Corinthians 12-14) reveal that these special manifestations were given to certain persons, for certain purposes, and in certain ways. So the passage in Mark must be qualified by asking, "About whom is the Lord speaking?" This makes a difference in our understanding of a given passage.

When Was It Spoken?

Too many Bible readers and teachers have far too little regard for this. Just to quote the Bible, any part of it, seems to cast a divine spell on their argument. Our last study in the different covenants should have convinced us of this folly. What a vast difference there is between a commandment given in Leviticus and one given in Acts, or a promise offered in Genesis and one in Romans.

Consider the most important question a person can ask, "What must I do to be saved?" And yet, people will go back and seek to enforce a commandment taken from an old covenant, which never even promised salvation from sin. This is the tragic error of being firmly convinced that the keeping of the Ten Commandments is sufficient for being assured of heaven.

The issue of "when," if properly weighed, will enable the student to have a far better understanding of the teachings of Jesus. Even though our Lord taught men in preparation for the new covenant, He Himself lived under the old covenant. He taught much about the law and fulfilled it. A good case in point is the story of the thief on the cross, to whom Jesus promised paradise (Luke 23:43). Our Lord could forgive a person as He so desired. This transpired before the gospel plan of salvation was given. After Jesus died, as the testator of a new will He could expect that the terms of that will be met. Our understanding then of the exact steps of salvation must be ascertained by studying those cases which followed the death of Jesus on the cross. "When" a passage was spoken or written bears heavily on its meaning.

Where Was It Spoken?

The Bible is a record of real people and actual happenings. Sometimes the difference between understanding a passage or misunderstanding it is nothing more than a matter of being willing to place it back in its local environment. Where it was spoken means something.

On one occasion when Jesus had healed a leper, He said to the man, "See that you don't tell anyone" (Matthew 8:4). On another occasion, after He had healed a man who had an unclean spirit, Jesus told the man, "Go home to your family and tell them how much the Lord has done for you, and how he has had mercy on you" (Mark 5:19).

Jesus' apparent contradictory actions in these two cases is readily understood when we realize that the healings took place in different locations. The first occurred in Galilee, where enthusiasm for Jesus ran at a high pitch. The report of a miracle, had it been widely heralded, might have brought this enthusiasm to the boiling point, seriously disrupting Jesus' ministry. The second miracle occurred among the Gadarenes, where Jesus' ministry had scarcely touched. Thus a wide publication of the miracle would have helped rather than hindered His future ministry among the people of Gadara. In other words, "where" an even occurs may have a great deal of bearing on its meaning.

When Jesus said, "It is easier for a camel to go through the eye of a needle than for a rich man to enter the kingdom of God" (Matthew 19:24), the place is Palestine. A camel was the largest beast in the land. Hence, for such to go through the eye of a needle was a strong figure of speech, denoting absolute impossibility. Or, another explanation provided by some is that a "needle's eye" was an oriental gateway or narrow door. Thus, such a large beast had to be unloaded of his burdens and then he had to creep through on his knees. This teaches that it is impossible to be saved by one's riches. Both pictures are very similar in meaning and they are most expressive when viewed in the light of the land where this was spoken.

What Were the Circumstances?

We must be careful never to isolate a passage. If we take it away from its setting, it will often be incomplete, even misleading. We must seek to enter fully into the experience of the writer or speaker, and see all the circumstances surrounding the passage under study. Learn to be inquisitive and curious about all conditions and circumstances.

For example, when we are confronted with the word "Samaritan," it is well to look thoroughly at its meaning. We discover it refers to a racially mixed people, part Jew and part Gentile, who lived right in the heart of Palestine. We also learn that the Jewish and Samaritan hatred for each other was steeped in history and tradition. From this alone we understand more fully the meaning of the parable, "The Good Samaritan." How significant was this one single factor of Jesus choosing the example of a Samaritan to answer the question, "Who is my neighbor?" (Luke 10:25-37).

In any passage try to ascertain the general subject or theme being discussed, as well as all the separate circumstances of the text. They blend together and complement each other.

Why?

Finally, seek to find out why the passage was written or spoken. What is the purpose or aim? Every God-given word is motivated by a reason and with an end in view. These purposes vary in nature. The purpose for writing the Gospel of Matthew was not at all the same as that for recording the Epistle to the Romans — and neither of these were prompted in the same way as was the book of Revelation. The same is true of individual passages.

An example of failing to clearly identify the aim of a passage is the use often made of Paul's teaching on the Lord's Supper, as found in 1 Corinthians 11:20-34. This, declare some, is Scriptural support for condemning the practice of serving any meals in the church building. But to argue in this fashion is to miss the point of Paul's admonition. In this passage Paul was condemning the excesses of eating and drinking that had come to be associated with the observance of the Lord's Supper in the Corinthian church.

There are many cases where the writer or speaker clearly states the purpose of his words, even for an entire book (Luke 1:1-4; John 20:30,31; 1 Timothy 3:14,15), or for separate passages (Luke 8:1-8; 9-15). However, there are many times when the general scope or aim of a passage will have to be determined by the context, and by putting the questions of this chapter into practice.

Questions for Review

1. What is meant by making an "historical approach" to a passage?
2. Name the seven questions that should be asked about any passage to be correctly understood.
3. Name several different classes of persons quoted in the Bible.
4. How can the Bible be divinely inspired, yet record things that are even untrue?
5. Show how a commandment and a promise intended for one person can entirely exclude another.
6. Why is it so important to determine when a thing was spoken?
7. In what two ways can the purpose of a passage be determined?

Assignment for Study

Study the words "I have sinned," as found in the following passages: Exodus 9:27; Numbers 22:34; Joshua 7:20; 1 Samuel 15:24; Job 7:20; Matthew 27:4; Luke 15:18. See what differences in meanings you can find simply by applying this rule on "correctly dividing the settings."

Topic for Discussion

Upon four separate occasions in the New Testament, that all-important question about salvation was asked by sinners, "What must I do?" (Matthew 19:16-21; Acts 2:21, 36-39; 16:29-33; 22:7-10, 16). Each received a different answer. Discuss in class how the application of the seven questions in this chapter can produce a harmonious understanding of them.

CHAPTER ELEVEN

The Types of Language Used

"Though I have been speaking figuratively, a time is coming
when I will no longer use this kind of language
but will tell you plainly about my Father"
(John 16:25).

In speaking to man God uses human language, the language man employs in his everyday life. He knows that "a word aptly spoken is like apples of gold in settings of silver" (Proverbs 25:11). Therefore the Lord has employed all the types of language known to man — from literal fact to figurative statement, prose to poetry, story to sermon, history to prophecy, and law to example. Each has its own nature, purpose, and method of understanding. Through such diversity, ranging from the literal to the figurative, we can be most effectively taught divine truth. This we do in everyday conversation. When did you last say, "I'm so tired, I'm dead," "I told her a thousand times," "He lost his head in anger," "I worked like a horse," "The car ate up the road," "Hold your horses," or "She's a dream"? These are nothing but figures of speech, entwined with literal facts, which we find useful in saying more expressly what we really mean.

Literal Language

Many, many times the Lord wished simply to state facts,

name persons and places, relate incidents, issue command-ments and warnings, or draw conclusions. Such things should be taken literally, just as we do in our daily conversations. There is a great area of communications best expressed in plain, literal facts. To be constantly searching for hidden meanings and fancy figures of speech would be useless. Too many Bible readers have forgotten this obvious truth, and so they exert wasteful and fruitless energy in forcing many liter-al words and expressions to issue forth with deep, spiritual meanings never intended. They don't interpret these, they explode them. Let us leave God's simple statements just as they are. Remember, a good portion of your Bible is plain, literal language.

Figurative Language

Even though God often expresses a truth in its usual sense (this is literal), frequently He uses a symbol, a story, or another more descriptive means (this is figurative). For example, it is literally true that God cares for us. And yet, how this truth is beautifully expressed with so much more impact by the well-known Twenty-third Psalm, with all its lovely figures of speech.

How can these two main types of language be correctly distinguished? How can one determine whether a passage is literal or figurative? How is this done in ordinary writings today? They are both common to human literature and daily speech. Should we not use the same common sense judg-ment? Simply stated, let us consider every passage as literal with the following exceptions:

1. When it involves an *impossibility* or an *absurdity*, it would be taken as figurative. Jesus said, "Let the dead bury their own dead" (Luke 9:60). The absurdity of a physically dead man going out and burying another dead man indicates that we must understand it as figurative language in order for this verse to make sense.

2. When it involves a *contradiction* or *inconsistency*. Again, Jesus said, "I am the resurrection and the life. He who

believes in me will live, even though he dies; and whoever lives and believes in me will never die" (John 11:25,26). If this is all literal, Jesus is contradicting himself.

3. When it involves an *immoral conclusion*. A good example here is the command of Jesus to cut off one's hand or foot, or pluck out one's eyes if such causes one to stumble (Matthew 18:8,9). Now God has always taught that it is a sin to mutilate the body. It would not only be morally wrong, but physically impossible, to carry out this command literally. Would not a person be a sorry sight were he to amputate each member of his body the first time it caused him to sin? This is a figure of speech teaching a basic principle in regard to temptation.

4. When it is otherwise *implied by the context* of the passage. In other words, after reading carefully the entire section of thought wherein such a passage is found, one can often ascertain from the general sense whether it is to be taken as literal or figurative.

5. When it is otherwise *stated*. Yes, the writer may come right out and say it is a figure of speech. Jesus boldly stood in Jerusalem and declared if they destroyed this temple, he would raise it up in three days. Now "this temple" was not Herod's temple where people worshiped, but He was using figurative language, foretelling the resurrection of His body — the writer says so (John 2:18-21).

6. When it is more apt to be figurative for the reason of sheer *common sense*. When Jesus promised to give the woman of Samaria "living water" (John 4:10-15), He was using highly figurative language to dramatically show this woman of sin and frustration what He really could do for her life.

Remember, unless any one of these six conditions is present, treat each passage as a simple, literal statement.

Purpose of the Figurative

Why use the figurative, when the literal is so plain?

Because figurative language can do some things that the literal cannot fully accomplish. It can add beauty, real adornment to plain truth; and it can illustrate and explain in its own peculiar way. Thus, facts become very much alive and warm. The truth often stands out more vividly and makes a more lasting impression on the mind and heart. The Bible says God loves us and longs to forgive us. But how much more abounding in meaning is this truth when Jesus tells the parable of the prodigal son.

Then too, sometimes God wants to teach us things that are outside of our experiences. Here we have no words in common, no vocabulary. How can God describe heaven (2 Corinthians 12:2-4)? It is to be a new experience. There will be things there we have never seen nor heard before. What is God to do but use symbols and figurative words so that we will get a true impression, as much as is possible? The figurative language ties together the seen and the unseen.

So the real purpose of the figurative language is not to teach new truth, but to illustrate and graphically portray truth taught elsewhere in Scripture. It must then *always be in harmony* with the literal facts. It will then help to make the truth vitally interesting and more easily remembered.

Rules for Understanding the Figurative

Great care must be taken in handling figurative language. It is not too difficult, for it always has been used in literature, especially among oriental writings. It is not just for the scholar, but such pictures are for the common man. When one speaks of a "cold heart" or a "warm heart" or a "soft heart," such figures of speech are clear and expressive. Now, what commonplace rules should we then employ in order to understand correctly the figurative language of the Bible?

1. Determine what *kind of figure* it is. There are several which will be discussed in the next section.

2. Next, follow the *author's explanation*, if he gives one. This is safe, because it is the inspired interpretation. When

Jesus gave the parable of the sower, He explained the figure of the seed as being the "word of God" (Luke 8:11). And in Luke 12:16-21, Jesus explained the basic meaning of an entire parable.

3. Be sure to *harmonize the figurative with the literal.* Remember, the purpose of the figurative is to complement, help, and illustrate the plain facts of truth. Never permit an interpretation to go off on some tangent. Keep it on course with Bible facts.

4. Be sure to *harmonize the figurative with the customs of the times.* If you were reading Shakespeare, you would want to understand his masterful pictures as he knew them and intended them. The Bible uses many figures typical of its own times of writing. It would be well for you to understand the "wedding feast" customs before determining the meaning of Jesus' likening the "kingdom of heaven" to "ten virgins" (Matthew 25:1-13). Another good example is the use of the term "dogs" when referring to wicked persons (Revelation 22:15; Psalm 59:6). In those days, dogs were, for the most part, undesirable pests which ran wild in the country, only to raid the cities for food by night, snarling and fighting.

5. Moreover, *do not press the meaning too far.* There is a temptation in dealing with the figurative to allow the imagination to run wild — to press all the details too far. Often there are incidentals in a figure which only serve to complete the picture. Concentrate on the main point or purpose. This is especially true of a parable. Do not feel bound to find a special significance in every detail.

6. Finally, remember that *figures of speech change.* They change their meaning from one instance to another. Such figures as fire, bread, water, and sheep do not always represent the same things. For example, the word "yeast" was once used as a symbol for the "kingdom of heaven" (Matthew 13:33), and in another instance Jesus used it to depict the evil teachings of the Pharisees and Sadducees (Matthew 16:6-12).

Figures of Speech

At this point, it would be well for the student to clearly identify the different kinds of figures of speech. These are used in ordinary literature, and God has employed the same tools for His purpose. We shall not endeavor to list every type. However, we do want to catalog the most common ones, define them, and provide some references as to where they may be found.

1. *Parable:* a simple, normal, real life story or illustration used to present some moral truth. The Scriptures record at least thirty parables that Jesus used during His ministry, such as the good Samaritan (Luke 10:25-37), the prodigal son (Luke 15:11-32), and the Pharisee and the tax collector (Luke 18:9-14). A parable had a way of concealing truth from those who would not receive or follow it (Matthew 13:10-16), while dramatically revealing it to those eager to listen and trust.

2. *Fable:* similar to a parable, but made up of a fictitious or imaginary story. Its purpose is to teach some moral lesson. It might designate some inanimate object as speaking (2 Kings 14:8-10).

3. *Simile:* a thing or action that is said to be "like" or "as" something of a different kind or quality. You often read such expressions as, "the Spirit of God descending like a dove" (Matthew 3:16), "though your sins are like scarlet, they shall be as white as snow" (Isaiah 1:18), and "we all, like sheep, have gone astray" (Isaiah 53:6).

4. *Metaphor:* a word or phrase which is said to be something else because of a likeness involved. It is simply calling one thing by another word, more descriptive and figurative. Jesus said of Herod, "Go tell that fox" (Luke 13:32). And in the upper room He said, "Take and eat; this is my body" (Matthew 26:26).

5. *Allegory:* a metaphor extended into a complete story to illustrate some truth. The writer does not identify all the particular parts, but leaves the reader to infer their meaning.

Paul's picture of the Christian putting on his armor for the battle of life is an excellent example (Ephesians 6:11-17).

6. *Riddle:* an analogy written up as a puzzle. To unravel it will thus produce some truth, as in Judges 14:14.

7. *Hyperbole:* an exaggeration of some statement for the purpose of emphasis. Notice the extreme statements in Psalm 22:6,14, spoken in such a manner for effect.

8. *Irony and sarcasm:* a sharp remark uttered in contempt or ridicule. These two words are basically the same, the latter being more severe in degree and intensity. A typical case of this is the taunting mockery which the soldiers threw into the face of Jesus just before He was crucified (Matthew 27:29), and which the chief priests and scribes cried out later on as He hung on the cross (Mark 15:31,32).

9. *Interrogation:* to question for effect, often not seeking an answer. Such a method will bring out a point very strongly, or even argue to the contrary, simply by the way in which the question is asked. Read Hebrews 2:3 and notice that to ask the question is to answer it with deadly force.

10. *Metonymy:* to substitute one word for another, because they are related. Let us explain. When Jesus spoke of "the cup" (1 Corinthians 11:25,26), He was referring to what was in the cup. Or when we read that "Moses . . . is read in the synagogues on every Sabbath" (Acts 15:21), it means that the word "Moses" is used for the writings of Moses.

11. *Personification:* a figure where inanimate beings have personal attributes. Read Psalm 114:3, "The sea looked and fled."

12. *Anthropomorphism:* the ascribing of human forms or attributes to God. The Bible speaks of the "hands," "back," and "face" of God (Exodus 33:22,23).

Four Peculiar Forms

Finally, let us note four peculiar types of language that make great use of the figurative as well as the literal. These are quite common in the Bible.

1. *Poetry*. This is the use of artistic and imaginative ideas expressed in a language of rhythm. Figures of speech and emotional expressions abound in Bible poetry — such as Psalms and Job.

2. *Proverb*. Here we have a profound but short pithy statement of truth, commonly held and valuable to those who will heed. The Bible has many of these, with the book of Proverbs most well known. A good example is one commonly quoted from Jesus' lips, "It is more blessed to give than to receive" (Acts 20:35).

3. *Prophecy*. This is any instruction from God to man in regard to some significant fact of the past, the present, or the future. The prophet thus declares vital truth that was, is, or is to be for the purpose of making man more aware of God's providential work in the world, His law, and how man should react to it. It is the element of future prediction that needs special care in interpretation. No doubt the predictions concerning the coming of Christ are the best known (Isaiah 9:6,7; 55:1-12; Micah 5:2).

A few warnings about this are in order. Never forget that predictions are divine and that they have a definite holy purpose. Watch for the fulfillment of prophecies stated elsewhere in Scripture (Joel 2:28-32 in Acts 2:17-21; Isaiah 53:7,8 in Acts 8:32,33). When this happens, you can be certain of the explanation; otherwise, do not forget you are not an infallible interpreter. Consider each prophecy in the light of its own setting and in harmony with all other Scripture. Remember that many have both an immediate and an ultimate (long-range) significance. Finally, recognize the many figures of speech used in issuing prophecies.

4. *Type*. Here we have a person, object, or incident, prefiguring something greater and more exalted that is to follow. Also, some moral principle is involved. For example, to teach one thing, Adam is said to be one type of Christ (Romans 5:14). Melchizedek was a type of Christ to illustrate another truth (Hebrews 7:17). Moreover, the Passover lamb was a

symbol of Christ for still another lesson (1 Corinthians 5:7; 1 Peter 1:19). Types were thus symbols of figures of something great. Sometimes these were things, offices, events, or places as well as persons.

Physical
Alike   Spiritual Alike

Questions for Review

1. Define literal and figurative language.
2. What are the purposes for speaking in the figurative?
3. One should always choose the literal interpretation of a passage unless what conditions are present?
4. Give the six rules important to the understanding of figurative language.

Assignment for Study

Listed below are the twelve types of figures of speech discussed in this lesson, along with as many Scripture selections illustrating these types. Match them correctly by drawing a line from the passage to the proper word.

Parable	Matthew 28:3
Fable	2 Samuel 1:23
Simile	1 Peter 4:18
Metaphor	Luke 14:15-24
Allegory	Matthew 10:34
Riddle	Habakkuk 3:10
Hyperbole	Matthew 5:13
Irony, Sarcasm	Ezekiel 17:3-21
Interrogation	Judges 9:8-20
Metonymy	1 Kings 18:27
Personification	Ruth 2:12
Anthropomorphism	Galatians 4:21-31

Topic for Discussion

Explain how you would describe "ice," in both literal and figurative language, to a simple native living near the equator. Show the power of the figurative.

CHAPTER TWELVE

Know the Meaning of Words and Sentences

"Retain the standard of sound words, which you have heard from me"
(2 Timothy 1:13, NASB).

Man uses his tongue, lips, teeth, throat, and lungs to issue forth sounds, which in turn are symbols of the thoughts in his mind. These, when put together in certain ways, are called words. Words are not things, but are symbols of things. John Locke once wrote, "We should have a great many fewer disputes in the world if words were taken for what they are, the signs of our ideas only, and not for things themselves." They are not vain sounds, nor are they ends in themselves.

Remember Shakespeare's famous character, Hamlet, who feigned madness? Polonius asked him, "What do you read, my Lord?" He replied, "Words, words, words." No, words are not so empty and meaningless as Hamlet's retort.

Suppose you were to hear a series of "dot and dash" sounds put together in such a way as to convey a definite message according to the Morse code. But you do not know this code. The sounds would therefore be meaningless. You would have an experience of hearing a chattering noise, not that of receiving an intelligent message. The symbols are not known by both you and the sender.

The same is true of words. They are signs of thoughts.

One person has a thought that he wants to pass on from his mind to yours. He simply fashions it into an appropriate, audible word. If this word is also familiar to you, and is a symbol of the same thought, then as you hear the word this thought passes from the speaker's mind to your mind. This is what takes place when you look in the dictionary for the meaning of an unknown word. You simply see what that word symbolizes as it is described by other symbols (words) that you do know.

If we want to know the exact meaning of God's Word, we certainly must know the exact meanings of the words God chose. Each one is a symbol of His thoughts. We are to "retain the standard of sound words" (2 Timothy 1:13). The word "standard" means a "model" or "pattern" that has definite size and shape for the purpose of maintaining a sameness in meaning. It is, therefore, exceedingly important that we correctly define all words. In this way we shall be able to understand what God has in mind.

As an example, let a student stand up in class and utter some statement of fact, a thought that he feels is previously unknown to the rest of the students. How do the others interpret what he said? Is there a difference or conflict in their understandings? If so, why? Are some of the words not clearly understood? Are they not held in common by all? Suppose this same statement were uttered somewhere else in the world, or one thousand years earlier in history, or one thousand years later, or to some other group of listeners. Would the meaning change? It is important for us to know the meanings of words exactly as God used them, so that His thoughts may flow freely and unpolluted into our minds.

The Meaning of Words

The process of defining words is that of making sure that we hold these words in common with God; that they symbolize to us exactly the same thought He wished to convey to us. In order to accomplish this, let us list the logical steps the student must take with all Bible words.

1. *Seek the original meaning of a word.* Frequently a person will look up the meaning of a Bible word in a standard American dictionary. This is not sufficient. We are not interested in the modern use of a word nor in the most popular opinion about it. If we are to understand the thought of God, we must know the meaning of that word He chose, as He chose it. Of course, it was in another language. The ideal thing would be for all of us to be proficient in Greek and Hebrew, as spoken at the time the Scriptures were written. This being impossible, at least improbable, the next best thing is to turn to reliable Bible dictionaries, extended translations, and commentaries. Generally, this is not hard to do and it proves most rewarding in cases of key words and significant meanings.

The real purpose here is to go back and see the words strictly from the viewpoint of the writers. Remember, when the Holy Spirit inspired men to write, He didn't, for the most part, pick out strange and new words. To the contrary, He directed the use of the ordinary, commonly used vocabulary of that time. Interpreting the message, then, is a matter of understanding each word in the usual or current meaning of that time — what anybody would ordinarily have thought of that word when it was used. We have no right to attach our own ideas to words and thus mistake the writer's meaning. He used words as he knew them. It is our job to know that meaning. This is not hard. Scholars have done a magnificent job for us. They have studied the languages, the peoples, the customs, the literature of those times, and have been able to exhume all the fine shades of meanings for us. We just need to take the trouble to search them out.

Words of all languages drift away from their original meanings. Time changes them. This process is presently going on in our own language. Some words we use today vary slightly in meaning from what they meant even a generation ago. And some words drop out of use altogether. The word "let" has completely reversed itself in the English language, between the time the Bible was translated in the days of King James (A.D. 1611) when it meant to "hinder" or "restrain," and the present time when it means to "allow" or "permit."

We must be careful lest we attach the present-day meaning of a Bible word that has undergone such a change. We are never justified in making words mean something other than what the writers originally intended them to mean. A good case in point, to illustrate this first step, is the often debated word, "baptism." In verb or noun form, it occurs one hundred and two times in the New Testament. It was a word commonly used in that time. Its meaning can be easily ascertained, even in secular writings, as having the simple action of dipping, washing, immersing, or burying an object in some kind of substance. The original intent is clear.

2. The next step is to remember that *each word in a given instance has but one meaning*. More and more Bible students are coming to realize that this is the truth. At times man has felt that the Bible was different, that its words were filled with two or more meanings. It became the duty of the really "spiritual" to find them all. Thus, many false doctrines were born.

No one uses words with double (or more) meanings unless he speaks in riddles, is ambiguous, or is guilty of duplicity. Suppose you were to arrive home and find a note left by a parent, or some other member of the family. Something very important suddenly came up, plans had to be abruptly changed, it was a grave matter concerning a loved one's safety, and the message was a simple word of direction. Would it be carefully written in words that give clear instruction? Would this be a time for sensible people to speak in riddles? When a person writes an important message that must be understood, he uses words that best serve to allow exactly what he thinks to flow into the mind of the reader. He doesn't want anyone to draw any meanings other than the ones he wishes to impart. Each word is chosen because it contains the one construction of ideas he is thinking. He resents anyone who toys loosely with his words and imposes a collection of meanings on them. This is misrepresentation.

Doesn't God have definite ideas (life and death matters) that He is eager and able to impart to us through human language? This is the Bible.

3. Sometimes the writer takes the time to define his own terms, *and his definition is always best.* It is a self-evident fact that anyone has the right to use whatever words he chooses, as long as he makes them plain and defines what he means. After all, he knows what he is trying to say better than anyone else.

Sometimes people quote Romans 14:23 as proof that it is sinful not to believe in God, for Paul says, "Everything that does not come from faith is sin." It is true that one should have faith in the Lord, but this is not the Scripture to use. Read the entire chapter and note that the writer is using the word "faith" in a different sense. It is not disbelief in God as such. This is a case in which one who eats meat, believing that he ought not to do it, is thus doing wrong. He is violating his conscience. Even though it is a matter of opinion, he sins if he honestly believes he ought not do this.

4. The next problem to be faced concerning words is the fact that *many words have more than one meaning.* This is not surprising. Look at our English words. The dictionary lists at least fifteen meanings for the word "flesh," twelve for "life," and thirty-one for "cross." This fact, of course, furnishes the seedbed for much of our American humor. The same is true of many Greek and Hebrew words. Sometimes there are fine shades of meaning that prove very significant. So as such a word is approached in Scripture, how may the reader determine just which meaning the author intended? There are several simple ways in which this can be done.

a. In the first place, it would always be wise to use that shade of meaning currently in use at the time of writing. It would be foolish to permit a word used by the apostle John to embody a thought that was not born until five hundred years after he lived.

b. Then look at the context where the word is found. This is one of the biggest aids. As subjects vary, so do the uses of words. We do this every day ourselves. We use the same words over and over, meaning different things, according to what we are talking about at the time. We say, "cross the street," "she is cross this afternoon," and "Jesus died on the cross," all being quite different. The meaning of "hate" as used in 1 John 3:14,14 is "rancor" or "animosity," while in Luke 14:26 an alternate meaning of "loving less" seems demanded by the very nature of the discussion. Never forget this lesson. It is plain common sense and will mean so much to your understanding of the Bible.

Here is a simple test that can be made. If there is any doubt as to which meaning to use, substitute the various definitions in place of the word itself. The one shade that seems to fit the passage best will often come to light by this practice. This helps immeasurably. As a matter of fact, this proves most useful even when there is but one meaning to a word. Put the definition of a word right in its place in any given verse. Watch it become more alive.

c. Sometimes the right shade of meaning for a word can be determined by observing closely the purpose of the writer, or the general scope of the writing. What is the writer intending to say or prove? What is the basic idea or theme of the book? The main idea of the Epistle to the Romans is quite different from that of James. This reflects greatly on some of the words each uses — the word "faith" is a good example. Never lose sight of the main topic of a book.

d. Then make good use of the practice of comparison. Consult similar or parallel passages where the same word occurs, and see how it is being used — especially passages in the same book. In any such comparison, always keep in mind that fundamental principle of the harmony of all Scripture.

No shade of meaning should be accepted if it violates this principle. For instance, we read in Exodus 10:20 that the Lord hardened the heart of Pharaoh. Never force the meaning to contradict the Bible doctrine of God's patience, mercy, and desire for man to repent. God hardens the heart that wants to be hardened by the truth.

5. The final step in determining the meaning of words is to *recognize some words as having a specific Biblical meaning.* What is meant by this? Every field of learning has its own special vocabulary — chemistry, golf, mathematics, music, politics, etc. Each has its own technical words. So has the Bible.

This is the way it works. God chose a general (generic) word to convey the long-desired nature of the coming system of the Christian faith and hope. So He selected a common word, "good news," which is often translated "gospel" in the New Testament. By doing so, God makes it to refer to the specific good news of salvation: the life, death, burial, and resurrection of Jesus Christ (1 Corinthians 15:1-4). Therefore, when the Bible student encounters this word in his reading, he realizes that it is not just any kind of good news, but specifically that news concerning the Lord and what it means to him. This is purely the Bible usage of this particular term, and should be so understood. Other examples of special Bible terms are conversion, saint, church, deacon, elder, apostle, fellowship, repent, and faith. These, and many more, have special Biblical meanings.

The Meaning of Sentences

Now that we have ascertained the meaning of individual words, let us put them together in a definite arrangement so that they compose a unit of thought. This is a sentence. A sentence is like a bridge — even though it is composed of carefully designed parts, unless they are correctly put together, the whole is apt to be weak and may collapse. It is most essential that we give as much attention to the arrangement of words as we do their selection and meaning. The arrangement can greatly affect the meaning. Let us list two important steps in determining the meaning of sentences.

1. *Observe all the simple rules of grammar and rhetoric.* Is this not common sense? Diagram (at least mentally) the subject, predicate, and modifiers of a sentence. Watch the punctuation. Observe the weight of verb tenses and moods of sentences. Note the use of prepositions, personal pronouns, and definite articles. Now for some examples.

How many people have read 1 Corinthians 11:27 and concluded that they are too unworthy to partake of the Lord's Supper? This misunderstanding is based on the failure to follow a simple rule of grammar. Notice, the word "unworthily" (in the King James Version) is an adverb, not an adjective. An adjective modifies a noun, but an adverb modifies a verb, an adjective, or another adverb. As an adverb, it modifies "shall eat" and not "whosoever." So it is not the person who is unworthy, but the manner of partaking. This happens to be the theme of the whole context (vv. 20-34) in the first place. The NIV properly translates it "in an unworthy manner."

A case of a frequent violation of the rules of rhetoric is found in Matthew 16:18. It has been advocated that Peter is the rock upon which the church is founded. What is the picture given here by our Lord? The church is a building and Christ is the builder. Then is Peter the foundation? No. He is the doorkeeper, and he cannot be both doorkeeper and foundation. Besides, the meanings of the words prevent this. The Greek word translated "Peter" means a "stone," a "loose stone," but the word for "rock" means "a rocky ledge, solid rock." Jesus is not making a comparison, but a contrast. The church is not founded on a man, but on something stronger and more lasting. What then is this rock? What is left? Apparently the great confession of faith in Jesus Christ (v. 16), which Peter had just made and which Jesus had just declared was revealed from God. This is good rhetoric.

2. *Put to use all the rules of comparison* as advocated in the case of individual words. Remember what was already men-

tioned? Compare each sentence with the context in which it is found, with the general scope and purpose of the entire writing, and with other passages on similar themes. Sentences must be carefully related to other portions of Scripture in the same manner as words.

Questions for Review

1. What is meant by saying words are symbols of things or ideas?
2. Why is it important to define words correctly?
3. Name the five steps one should take in order to determine the correct meaning of a word.
4. What is meant by the "original" meaning of a word? Does the original meaning of a word ever change?
5. Why is a writer's own definition of a word best?
6. Can you name ways to determine exactly which shade of meaning of a word is correct?
7. Why is it important to obey the rules of grammar in studying sentences?

Assignment for Study

To draw a contrast between the original and present-day use of the word "baptism," list all the meanings in several English dictionaries, and in as many Greek dictionaries as you can obtain.

Topic for Discussion

Have several in the class take turns showing how God has taken a general word and given it a specific Biblical meaning of its own.

CHAPTER THIRTEEN
The Limit of Divine Revelation

". . . so that you may learn from us the meaning of the saying, 'Do not go beyond what is written'"
(1 Corinthians 4:6).

The final lesson to be learned is just where the Bible ends. There is a limit, a stopping place of God's Word. This is the point where the Lord ends His revelation. Many students fail to locate this and so add greatly to their misunderstanding of the Bible.

A man draws up a will. In it are certain specifications, promises, restrictions, etc. The terms are clear. But then, when the author has said exactly all that he wants to say, he stops. This is the end of his will. An observer might list a hundred things that the will failed to say. But these unsaid things never came from the author. They are merely private opinions of a reader. By intelligent study one can determine the exact limit separating what he said and what was unsaid.

This must be done with the Scriptures. We must be able to ascertain the exact limit of all that God has said. Anything beyond this would merely be the opinion of man. This is one of the main reasons why many of the scribes and Pharisees failed to understand Jesus. They had confused divine wisdom with human wisdom. They had failed to see where the one left off and the other began. So the Master remarked, "They worship me in vain; their teachings are but rules taught by men" (Matthew 15:9).

On any given statement, God has either spoken or He has not spoken. Both cannot be true. This is obvious. Suppose you are a relative of someone who has made a will. Either you are in the will as a beneficiary or you are not. It cannot be both.

So it is with any single part of any Scripture passage you might consider. Either God has revealed His will in it or He has not. It is exceedingly important for a Bible student to learn to determine the difference. He must never become wise beyond that which is written.

The Spoken Area

The first duty then is to learn all that God has spoken. This is the great "thus says the Lord" area. Anything at all in this area we might call a "matter of faith." By this we mean that whenever the Lord speaks we simply trust His judgment, we believe His Word, and we completely submit our thoughts to His. We have no right to project our opinions into areas where God has clearly revealed His will. As we proceed, study carefully these thoughts as illustrated in the chart opposite.

Basically, there are two ways in which God has spoken to us in His Word. Sometimes He tells us and at other times He shows us. Let us examine both:

1. *Precept.* This is "any commandment, instruction, or order intended as an authoritative rule of action." When God tells us anything, we must try to grasp it and then surrender to its every demand. It may be in the form of:

A simple fact to believe;

A positive command to obey;

A prohibition to keep;

A promise to accept;

A warning to heed.

Whatever the form, man has no right to argue, ignore, or toy with a "thus says the Lord." Alexander Campbell once wrote,

FAITH *versus* OPINION

Facts

GOD HAS NOT SPOKEN

Man is challenged to discover unrevealed truth

PRECEPTS

Faith

GOD HAS SPOKEN

PRECEDENTS

UNWISE OR IMPROPER

Opinions

GOD HAS NOT SPOKEN

Man is free to fashion his own personal opinions

The Christian institution has its facts, its precepts, its promises, its ordinances, and their meaning or doctrine. These are not matters of policy, of arrangement, of expediency, but of divine and immutable ordination and continuance. Hence the faith, the worship, and the righteousness, or the doctrine, the piety, and the morality of the gospel institution, are not legitimate subjects of human legislation, alteration, or arrangement. No man nor community can touch these and be innocent. These rest upon the wisdom and authority of Jehovah; and he that meddles with these presumes to do that which the cherubim and seraphim dare not. Whatever, then, is a part of the Christian faith or the Christian hope — whatever constitutes ordinances or precepts of worship, or statutes of moral right and wrong, like the ark of the covenant, is not to be touched with uninspired and uncommissioned hands.[1]

Thus, where the Bible speaks, we must speak. We dare do nothing other than this. At times we may be tempted to insert our own judgment or alter the spoken word in favor of our own opinion — but, God forgive, these things ought not to be. We only have to use all of our powers of reason to ascertain exactly what God has spoken, and leave it at that.

2. *Precedent.* This is "something done or said that may serve as an example to authorize a subsequent act of the same kind." In other words, God often felt it more effective to show something than to tell it. He did this through the lives of people, deeds done, and examples given. Many Bible students have failed to see the weight of this kind of teaching. For example, Jesus gave no specific commandment for Christians to meet on the first day of the week. Yet the precedent that the early church set while under the leadership of the inspired apostles is obvious (Acts 20:7; 1 Corinthians 16:2).

Sometimes certain happenings recorded were only incidental and never intended to be examples to be consistently

---

[1]Alexander Campbell, *The Christian System.* (Nashville, TN: Gospel Advocate Co., 1974 reprint of 2nd ed. 1839), p. 57.

followed in the years after. The meaning in each case must be ascertained. When there was divine approval of such an example being a model to follow, then we often term it as an "approved precedent." Precedents then must be correctly divided like anything else. Especially should the rules of chapter 10 be used in order to do this correctly.

A good example of the power of precedent may be found in regard to the subject of when to observe the Lord's Supper. Nowhere in the New Testament is there any precept on how often it is to be practiced. Even 1 Corinthians 11:26 does not help, for this is not a discussion of the frequency but of the manner of partaking. So we next turn to precedent. Here we find our answer. It becomes quite clear that the New Testament church, under the direction of the inspired apostles, observed it on the first day of the week (Acts 2:42; 20:7).

So, precept and precedent complement each other to produce the total picture of God's revealed will. Having clearly identified and marked out the boundaries of these two implements, let the real students never go beyond and make any human demand as though it were the word of God. We must, as Thomas Campbell once declared,

> reduce to practice the simple, original form of Christianity expressly exhibited upon the sacred page; without attempting to inculcate anything of human authority, of private opinion, or inventions of men, as . . . matter of Christian . faith, or duty, for which there cannot be expressly produced a "thus saith the Lord" either in express terms, or by approved precedent.[2]

The Silent Area

How is this area determined? It is a matter of simple logic. Enclose all the area where God has spoken: everything else is

---

[2]Thomas Campbell, "Declaration and Address." (Lincoln, IL: Lincoln Christian College Press, 1971 reprint of 1809 edition), pp. 3,4.

obviously the silent area.

It is unthinkable to imagine that God would do all of man's thinking for him. Surely one made in God's image would be permitted to do as much of his own thinking as the Lord knows would be safe and wise. Refer back to the chart on page 137. Actually there are two kinds of knowledge that man is free to obtain on his own: (1) There are countless numbers of facts that man is challenged and expected to discover by his own ingenuity and scientific process. These are the everyday, but nevertheless intriguing, fields of the physical and social sciences. (2) The other type of thinking is common personal opinion. Differences of opinion are most natural to life; therefore this indeed is a vast area. Old "Raccoon" John Smith once said, "While there is but one faith, there may be ten thousand opinions."

Name any phase of any subject and you will notice that it must fall in either the "spoken" (Faith) area or the "silent" (opinion) area. It cannot be both. Either God has revealed His will or not. Let us take a general subject, that of prayer. Watch how different aspects of this important doctrine fall into one or the other of two areas: (1) In the field of *precept* it is positively commanded of every Christian (Ephesians 6:18; 1 Thessalonians 5:17; 1 Timothy 2:8; James 5:16). Further, *precedent* provides us a moving lesson of the power generated when the Christians met together and engaged in fervent and selfless prayer (Acts 4:23-37). (2) Then when it comes to the area of *opinion* look how much God did not say about this subject. For instance, consider the one issue of the posture of the body in prayer — opinions can and do vary. One could kneel, lie prostrate, sit, stand, walk, stoop, or bow down and still fulfill all that the Lord required of him. This leads us to that all-important point of respecting this right of opinion. If God permitted man an area in which to exercise his own opinion, as long as he does not violate any "thus says the Lord" in doing so, then no one has the right to deny him that privilege. This is a precept in itself (Romans 14; 1 Corinthians 8,9; Colossians 2:16). This is why we say, "Where the Scriptures speak, we speak [we have no right to do anything else when God speaks], and where the Bible is silent, we are silent [we dare not demand that which God has left free by His silence]." The Lord, in the fourteenth chapter of Romans, has left us some very important teaching on how we should behave in the use of our own opinions and our attitude toward the opinions of others.

Now may we offer some words of caution. First of all, it is easy to misuse our opinions. We can actually violate the will of the Lord with them. This is not right. This is exactly what the scribes and Pharisees were doing. Jesus was not so much concerned about changing their opinions. Rather, He sought to expose the fact that they were actually disobeying God's law by the way in which they were exercising their opinions (Matthew 15:3).

Then, too, sometimes our opinions can be either *inexpedient* (unwise — 1 Corinthians 6:12; 10:23) or *improper* (Romans 14:22,23). These we have indicated on the chart by the casting of a shadow over a part of the field of opinion. Certain conditions in life sometimes prevail to make this so. An example of the first was Paul's decision not to marry simply because, due to circumstances prevailing at that time, it would have been unwise for him (1 Corinthians 7:26-31; 9:5). And in the case of one having a conscience against eating meats that had been set aside for pagan worship, even though one did not so worship, it would have been bad to go ahead and eat if he honestly felt it improper to do so (Romans 14:22,23).

One must be careful about making *inferences* from Scripture. This is where much misunderstanding of the Bible arises. There is a difference between the clear statements of the Word and any conclusions we draw from them. An inference actually is a conclusion that one feels is right and intended by God, even though not stated. In order to clarify this we should note that there are three kinds of inferences:

(1) *Necessary* inferences — those made necessary by the passages involved.

(2) *Feasible* inferences — those which are logically probable, but not necessary.

(3) *Arbitrary* inferences — those chosen out of several probable alternatives, one being as good as another. (Note, however, that people may differ in their judgment of whether an inference is necessary, feasible, or arbitrary.)

Take baptism as an example of all three. After studying all the requirements for being baptized it is a necessary inference that infants cannot be Scripturally baptized, simply because they cannot fulfill the baptism requisites of faith and repentance. Next, it is a feasible inference that all the people baptized in Jerusalem on the Day of Pentecost (Acts 2) in all probability (but not of necessity) used the various pools of the city. And, it would become an arbitrary inference when a person seeks a preference as to a certain type of water (pool, river, etc.) for his own baptism, after observing the baptisms of the New Testament. One can readily see that the first (necessary inference) carries by far the most weight. But always be careful with any inference. In this, one is subject to error of judgment.

A Simple Test

In closing this important study may we suggest the following test as a great help in understanding this lesson. All issues can be divided into three categories:

1. *Scriptural* — that thought which has been revealed in Scripture, either by precept or precedent. This can be determined by honest study.

2. *Unscriptural* — (the prefix "un" means "not") that which has not been revealed in Scripture. It simply means it is not in the Bible. God never said to do it, believe it, or not to do it. He simply never said anything about it. It is a negative term.

3. *Antiscriptural* — (the prefix "anti" means "opposite,

against") that which violates the Scriptures. This could involve either of the above issues. One could do a Scriptural thing in a way that would violate the Scriptures. In the Sermon on the Mount, Jesus showed this in regard to praying (Matthew 6:5-8) and giving (Matthew 6:1-4). Or one could violate the Scriptures by the way he holds or uses an unscriptural issue. Man has every right to eat or drink anything he wishes, unless it violates the Scriptural law of love, which he must have for his brother (Romans 14:13-17). Keep these issues clear and your understanding of the Bible will be greatly increased.

Questions for Review

1. Why is it important to know the exact limit of divine revelation?
2. What is meant by the "spoken" area and the "silent" area?
3. What are the two basic ways God has spoken through the Scriptures? Explain them.
4. How may opinions fail to be expedient or proper?
5. What is meant by an inference? Name three kinds of inferences used in Bible study.
6. Explain the simple threefold test mentioned in the latter part of the chapter.

Assignment for Study

Explain the meaning of the following:
1. "Where the Scriptures speak, we speak, and where the Bible is silent, we are silent."
2. "Matters of faith and matters of opinion."
3. "While there is but one faith, there may be ten thousand opinions."

Topic for Discussion

Select different doctrinal subjects (such as church, prayer, worship, stewardship, etc.) and discuss them in class, showing how different phases of each fall into the category of either "faith" or "opinion."

Bibliography

Prepared by Lynn Gardner, Academic Dean of Ozark Christian College.

I. Books on Interpretation by authors from Restoration Heritage

Campbell, Alexander. *Christianity Restored.* Rosemead, CA: Old Paths Book Club, 1959 reprint of 1835 ed.

_____ . *The Christian System.* Nashville: Gospel Advocate Co., 1974 reprint of 2nd ed. of 1839.

_____ . "The Sermon on the Law" in *Millennial Harbinger,* 1846, pp. 493ff., in *Historical Documents Advocating Christian Union* ed. by C.A. Young. Joplin, MO: College Press, 1985.

Cottrell, Jack. *Solid.* Joplin, MO: College Press, 1991 (originally published by Baker under the title *The Authority of the Bible.*

Dungan, D.R. *Hermeneutics.* Delight, AR: Gospel Light, 1888.

Ensign, Grayson Harter. *You Can Understand the Bible.* Amarillo, TX: G and E Press, 1990.

Foster, Lewis. "Biblical Interpretation," *Restoration Herald* (Nov. 1956–Jan. 1959), Cincinnati, OH.

_____ . "Biblical Interpretation and Contemporary Thought," *Restoration Herald* (May 1968–Dec. 1969), Cincinnati, OH.

_____ . *Selecting a Translation of the Bible.* Cincinnati, OH: Standard, 1983.

Kearley, F. Furman, Edward P. Myers, and Timothy Hadley, eds. *Biblical Interpretation.* Grand Rapids: Baker, 1986.

Lamar, J.S. *The Organon of Scripture.* Philadelphia: J.B. Lippincott and Company, 1859: reprinted Rosemead, CA: The Old Paths Book Club, 1952.

Lockhart, Clinton. *Principles of Interpretation.* Delight, AR: Gospel Light, 1901.

Milligan, Robert. *Reason and Revelation.* Rosemead: Old Paths Book Club, 1953.

Palmer, W. Robert. *What the Bible Says About Faith and Opinion.* Joplin, MO: College Press, 1980.

Stroop, J. Ridley. *Why Do People Not See the Bible Alike?* Nashville: 20th Century Christian, 1949.

Thomas, J.D. *We Be Brethren.* Abilene, TX: Biblical Research Press, 1958.

Wilson, Seth and Lynn Gardner. *Learning from God's Word.* Joplin, MO: College Press, 1989.

II. Selected books on Interpreting the Bible

Berkhof, Louis, *Principles of Biblical Interpretation.* Grand Rapids: Baker, 1950.

Black, David A. *Linguistics and New Testament Interpretation.* Nashville: Broadman, 1992.

Bruce, F.F. *History of the Bible in English: From the Earliest Versions.* New York: Oxford University Press, 1978.

Carson, D.A. *Biblical Interpretation and the Church: Text and Context*. Grand Rapids: Baker, 1988.

_____ and John D. Woodbridge, eds. *Scripture and Truth*, rev. ed. Grand Rapids: Baker, 1992.

Conyers, A.J. *How to Read the Bible*. Downers Grove: InterVarsity, 1986.

Dockery, David S. *Biblical Interpretation Then and Now*. Grand Rapids: Baker, 1992.

Fee, Gordon D. and Douglas Stuart. *How to Read the Bible for all its Worth*, 2nd ed. Grand Rapids: Zondervan, 1993.

Finzel, Hans. *Unlocking the Scriptures: A Fresh New Look at Inductive Bible Study*. Wheaton: Victor, 1986.

_____ and Patricia Picardi. *Observe, Interpret, Apply*. Wheaton: Victor, 1986.

Green, Joel B. *How to Read the Gospels and Acts*. Downers Grove: InterVarsity, 1978.

_____ . *How to Read Prophecy*. Downers Grove: InterVarsity, 1984.

Kaiser, Walter and Moises Silva. *An Introduction to Biblical Hermeneutics*. Grand Rapids: Zondervan, 1994.

Kaiser, Walter. *Back Toward the Future*. Grand Rapids: Baker, 1989.

_____ . *Toward an Exegetical Theology: Biblical Exegesis for Preaching and Teaching*. Grand Rapids: Baker, 1980.

Klein, William W., Craig L. Blomberg, and Robert L. Hubbard. *Introduction to Biblical Interpretation*. Dallas: Word, 1993.

Kuhatschek, Jack. *Taking the Guesswork out of Applying the Bible*. Downers Grove: InterVarsity, 1990.

Larkin, William J., Jr. *Culture and Biblical Hermeneutics*. Grand Rapids: Baker, 1988.

McCartney, Dan and Charles Clayton. *Let the Reader Understand.* Wheaton: Victor, 1994.

McQuilkin, J. Robertson. *Understanding and Applying the Bible,* rev. ed. Chicago: Moody Press, 1992.

Ramm, Bernard. *Protestant Biblical Interpretation.* 3rd ed. Grand Rapids: Baker, 1970.

Sproul, R.C. *Knowing Scripture.* Downers Grove: InterVarsity, 1977.

Sterrett, T. Norton. *How to Understand Your Bible,* rev. ed. Downers Grove: InterVarsity, 1974.

Triana, Robert A. *Methodical Bible Study.* Grand Rapids: Zondervan, 1985.

Zuck, Roy B. *Basic Bible Interpretation.* Wheaton: Victor, 1991.

SAMPLE LIST OF TOOLS

CONCORDANCES

Strong, James. *Exhaustive Concordance of the Bible*. New York/Nashville: Abingdon-Cokesbury Press, 1953.

Young, Robert. *Analytical Concordance to the Bible*. Grand Rapids: Eerdmans, 1970.

Note: both of these are based on the text of the King James Version. Exhaustive concordances using the Strong numbers are available for the New International and New American Standard versions.

BIBLE DICTIONARIES AND HANDBOOKS

Achtemeier, Paul J., Ed. *Harper's Bible Dictionary*. San Francisco: Harper & Row, 1985.

Alexander, David and Pat Alexander, Eds. *Eerdmans' Handbook to the Bible*. Grand Rapids: Eerdmans, 1973.

Douglas, J.D. and Merrill C. Tenney, Eds. *The New International Dictionary of the Bible*. Grand Rapids: Regency Reference Library, 1987.

Gentz, William H. *The Dictionary of Bible & Religion*. Nashville: Abingdon, 1986.

Halley, Henry H. *Halley's Bible Handbook*. Grand Rapids: Zondervan, 1955.

Vine, W.E. *An Expository Dictionary of New Testament Words*. Westwood, NJ: Revell, 1940.

BIBLE ENCYCLOPEDIAS

Bromiley, Geoffrey W. *The International Standard Bible Encyclopedia*. Four volumes. Grand Rapids: Eerdmans, 1988.

Fausset, A.R. *Bible Encyclopaedia and Dictionary: Critical and Expository*. Grand Rapids: Zondervan, 1960.

Printed in the United States
937100001B